Better Homes and Gardens®

OUTDOOR PROJECTS
YOU CAN BUILD

BETTER HOMES AND GARDENS BOOKS

Editorial Director: Don Dooley
Executive Editor: Gerald M. Knox
Art Director: Ernest Shelton. Asst. Art Director: Randall Yontz
Production and Copy Editor: David Kirchner
Building and Remodeling Editor: Noel Seney
Building Books Editor: Larry Clayton
Architectural Editor: Stephen Mead
Remodeling and Home Maintenance Editor: David R. Haupert
Building Ideas Editor: Douglas M. Lidster
Remodeling Ideas Editor: Dan Kaercher
Kitchens, Appliances, Home Management Editor: Joan McCloskey
Associate Editor: Kristelle Petersen
Graphic Designers: Harijs Priekulis, Faith Berven,
Sheryl Veenschoten, Rich Lewis

CONTENTS

INSTANT PROJECTS

It's not how much time or money you spend on the projects you make, but how professional they look when you're finished that really counts. An obvious word of advice, to be sure, but advice worth repeating, just the same. Some do-it-yourselfers buy the very best materials and use the finest tools, yet their projects don't have that "finished" appearance. Others seem to get good results every time they pick up a hammer.

The "instant projects" in this section are designed to make you into that second type of easy expert. None of them requires more than a few hours of your time to build, and they won't cost you an arm and a leg, either. Try your hand at several of them and make yourself an instant woodworking star.

QUICK-CHANGE PLANT STAND

As you can see, this is not your average, run-of-the-mill plant holder. This one showcases your favorite greenery in an attractive, unusual way. But it also lets you change and rearrange for an ever-different display of flowers.

1 Lay two of the 2x2 uprights parallel to each other on the floor, then lay one of the crossmembers perpendicular to the two 2x2s, about a third of the distance from the top. (Allow the crossmember to overlap the uprights by two inches.)

2 Top the crossmember on each side with another 2x2 upright.

3 Use C-clamps at each end to hold members in position.

4 Drill two ¼-inch holes diagonal to each other through all three thicknesses of both legs, then secure with carriage bolts.

5 Repeat steps 1-4 for the other end.

6 Lay the 2x6s side by side and carefully mark the location of holes for the pots, using the space between the boards as the center of the circle.

7 Cut holes with a saber saw.

8 Position the 2x6s on top of the uprights as shown in the photo, and nail the ends of each 2x6 to the 2x2 crossmember.

9 Finish with oil or stain.

Materials (for project shown):
2x2 redwood—12 ft.
  8 12 in.   2 16 in.
2x6 redwood—12 ft.
  2 72 in.
Eight carriage bolts, and weathering oil or stain.

HALF-TILE YARD LIGHTS

Whether you're lighting an outdoor area for safety or atmosphere, this trio will serve you well. And you don't have to be an electrical wizard to install them.

1 Paint the inside of the half-tiles white. Let dry completely.
2 Bury flared or bell ends of tiles about 6 inches into ground.
3 Position outlets behind tiles.
4 Screw floodlights into ceramic fixtures, then plug in fixtures.

Materials: 6-inch clay half-tiles, floodlights, portable outdoor outlets (with cords), ceramic fixtures, and white paint.

STAIR-STEP PLANTERS

These simple planters are ideal for those difficult-to-decorate corner spots, or for edging your porch, patio, or driveway. Fill them with potting soil for your bulbs, seeds, or foliage plants. Or, if you wish, simply set out potted flowers for an easily changed display.

1 Set tiles into ground at various depths so exposed tile heights are 6, 12, 18 inches, etc.
2 Fill tiles with soil for planting, or with gravel for setting out potted plants.

Materials: 13-inch-square flue tiles 24 inches long.

FLUE TILE
BENCH

Sturdy, attractive, and easy to make—this bench satisfies all the prerequisites for a successful project. What's more, if you need storage space, you can use the tiles for stowing outdoor tools, games, or barbecue equipment.

1 Lay the seven redwood 2x4s side by side.

2 On top of these, place the two short 2x4s on edge 1½ to 2 feet apart (see photo). With fast-holding adhesive, glue these two crosspieces to the bench top and allow the adhesive to dry completely. No other means of attachment is necessary to secure this inviting seat top.

3 Carefully sand the top of the bench (to avoid splinters) and stain. For extra protection from the elements, apply a coat of varnish or shellac.

4 Position flue tiles in desired location on your patio.

5 Set bench top on flue liners, with the redwood 2x4 crosspieces butted against tiles to prevent any shifting.

6 To make an extra patio coffee table out of this unit, simply remove bench top from flue tiles, stand tiles on end, and replace top unit, adjusting the tiles so that crosspieces butt against the tiles to prevent shifting. The height of this quick-change table will be approximately 2 feet.

Materials (for project shown):
2x4 redwood—36 ft.
    7 54 in.
    2 24 in.
Two 13-inch-square chimney flue tiles (or liners), epoxy glue, and varnish or shellac.

ROUGH-HEWN FURNITURE

These benches and tables are as sturdy and rugged as any outdoor furniture you'll find. And they're particularly versa-tile because the design allows for a variety of arrangements on any patio or deck. Time needed to assemble?—just minutes!

1 Attach legs to 8x8 by centering a 2x4 a short distance from each end of timber (see photo at right). Nail 2x4s in place.
2 Invert 8x8 unit and position a 4x6 under each 2x4. Nail through 2x4 into 4x6. No other attachment is necessary.
3 Sand lightly, if desired. Finish bench with weathering oil or stain.

Materials (for each piece):
Fir lumber
   Length of 8x8
   2 2x4 10 in.
   2 4x6 12 in.
Weathering oil or stain.

INVITING DOOR KNOCKER

The striking good looks of this door knocker are unbeatable.

1 Cut three identical "club" shapes (see photo, right).
2 Drill a ¼-inch hole in "club" portion of two of the pieces and in "handle" portion of third.
3 Insert dowel pin through these holes (see photo for positioning).
4 Cut the "club" portion from reversed piece and glue it at base, between other pieces.
5 Stain. Glue knocker to door.

Materials: Three 10-in. 1x3s, one 3-in. dowel (¼ in. diameter), stain or weathering oil, and glue.

PLANT PEDESTALS

What could be a more ideal display for plants and greenery than a natural pedestal? The nice thing about these posts is that they become even more attractive as they weather.

1 Saw one large post (available at farm supply stores) into sections. Number and length of sections depend on your needs.
2 Decide upon desired effect and position each section.
3 Sink posts into concrete or leave positioned as is.
4 Set out your plants.

Materials: Posts (preferably 8 inches or more in diameter).

CANOPY BIRD FEEDER

1 Drill a ¼-inch hole in centers of hardboard and aluminum.
2 Butt-join the 1x2s; position and nail hardboard to this frame.
3 Slip rod through holes and secure with washers and nuts.
4 Drill four holes in each end of roof; screw to frame.
5 Bend rod. Hang with chain.

Materials (for project shown):
1x2 redwood—4 ft.
  2 10 in.   2 12 in.
One 12x12-inch piece ⅛-inch hardboard, one 25x12-inch sheet aluminum, ¼-inch threaded rod, washers, nuts, and chain.

TABLE IN THE ROUND

Fashioned from cedar or redwood and decorative concrete blocks, this sturdy piece of outdoor furniture is an inexpensive way to outfit your patio. The table shown here has a 48-inch diameter, but you can vary the size to fit your space requirements. Then use the same materials to build chairs, benches, and serving tables to complete your patio furnishings.

1 Mortar blocks together.
2 On large piece of paper, draw a 48-inch circle. Cut out circle.
3 Evenly cover the the circle with cedar or redwood on edge, about ½ inch apart.
4 Position the longer 1x4 perpendicularly across cedar. Glue. Nail crossmember to each cedar piece.
5 Place other two 1x4s about 9 inches on either side of secured crossmember. Nail these to cedar.
6 Invert top. Mark circle on cedar with pencil-string compass.
7 Cut tabletop along circle.
8 Place top on concrete blocks.

Materials (for a 48-inch diameter table):
1x2 cedar or redwood—120 ft.
1x4 cedar or redwood—10 ft.
  1 48 in.   2 36 in.
Six concrete blocks and mortar.

WINDOW WELL BENCH

1 Attach window well to the 2x4s with screws. (Drill extra holes in flange to put two screws in each end of 2x4.)
2 To give extra strength, insert a 2x4 on bottom edge. Secure with screws.
3 Finish with varnish.

Materials (for project shown):
2x4 redwood—28 ft.
  6 40 in.   1 36 in.
One 36-inch corrugated window well, wood screws, and varnish.

BURIED BIKE RACK

Tired of bikes scattered around your driveway and yard? Here's a rack that you hardly see until you need to use it. You can adjust the measurements given below to accommodate any number of bikes just by varying the spacing of the slats. What's more, you can build this bike rack to accept any size bike tire from the racy 10-speed to the balloon-tired bomber.

1 Decide on the location for your bike rack. It must be a spot that will allow for maneuvering bikes in and out of slots and around other parked bikes without damaging shrubbery, cars, or house siding.

2 Dig a 48x20-inch pit 6 inches deep.

3 To ensure adequate drainage, line pit with several inches of sand or fine gravel.

4 Treat all of the lumber with penta, a liquid preservative available at most hardware or lumber supply dealers. Allow the lumber to dry completely.

5 Cut 2x6s and 2x4s so that they fit snugly in the pit.

6 Construct the frame as indicated in the sketch at left.

7 Using two nails at each end, nail the slats to the frame allowing about ½ inch between them (refer to sketch at left). This spacing will vary, of course, depending on your needs.

8 Lower the rack into the pit.

9 Spread gravel or wood chips to brim of frames and slats around the bike rack. Or place two 24-inch-wide cement slabs flush to rack (to avoid the eventual scattering of gravel).

10 For protection against theft, lock bikes to rack by looping chains through tires and slats.

Materials (for project shown):
2x6 redwood—8 ft.
   2 48 in.
2x4 redwood—4 ft.
   2 17 in.
2x2 redwood—60 ft.
  30 20 in.
Penta and sand or fine gravel.

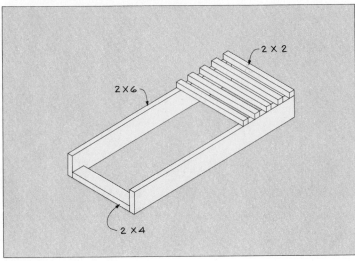

2 X 2
2 X 6
2 X 4

VERSATILE LATH CUBES

You can use this trio of sturdy lath cubes as planters, stools, storage units, end tables, coffee tables, or whatever the need dictates. Create a stair-step arrangement or align against that "problem" bare wall. The use and placement possibilities of these units are endless.

1 Cut the plywood side pieces, then glue and nail the sides of the box as shown in the sketch. (NOTE: Size of lath cubes can vary. When constructing foundation box, simply cut ½-inch plywood to dimensions that suit your needs. Adjust top and bottom accordingly.)

2 Cover each side with rough lath laid at 45-degree angles. Glue in place. Trim lath to fit.

3 To add bottom to cube, cut ½-inch plywood to fit. Glue and nail bottom into position.

4 Cut plywood top to fit. Glue strips of scrap lumber ⅜ inch from edges of underside. (These strips will keep the top in position, and at the same time allow you the flexibility of removing it.)

5 Sand top and shellac or paint a bright color. Apply stain or weathering oil to rest of unit.

6 To make unit into planter, cut hole the size of widest portion of pot so hole catches rim and holds pot in place.

Materials (for one cube):
½-in. exterior plywood—½ sheet
  2 14x14 in.   2 12½x14 in.
  2 13½x14 in.
¼-in. lath—51 ft.
Scrap lumber, exterior glue, and stain or weathering oil.

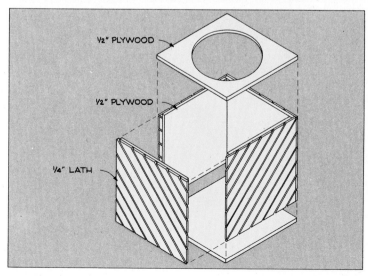

FREE-FORM MAILBOX

Here's a mailbox that you won't mind opening, even if you suspect there's a bill inside. It's a versatile project that allows you to add shelves and decorations as you see fit. You may want to use metal numbers on a suspended wooden plaque in lieu of the painted plaque shown here. Purchase bells to dangle from plaque or make your own from inverted clay pots.

1 Treat post with penta. Set post as directed on page 88.
2 Make a plywood box with hinge door (size depends on need).
3 Place two 1x4s horizontally to fit above mailbox and two to fit under. Nail to post. Insert box.
4 Place a 1x4 on each side of mailbox. Nail to horizontal pieces.
5 Nail additional pairs of horizontal beams to main post. For shelves, position 5-inch pieces of 1x4s across horizontal beams.
6 Apply stain or weathering oil.

Materials (for project shown):
4x4 redwood—8 ft.
1x4 redwood—21 ft.
 4 28 in. 2 18 in.
 2 21 in. 2 12 in.
¾-in. exterior plywood scraps, scrap 1x4, clay pots, one pair small butt hinges, penta, and stain or weathering oil.

TILE-LEGGED BENCH

1 Construct 1x4 frame.
2 Nail slats to frame, with about a ½ inch space between each.
3 Secure bell (large end) of tiles to bench with wood blocks.
4 Accent legs by painting stripes. Stain or paint bench.

Materials (for 6-foot bench):
1x4 redwood—50 ft.
 2 72 in. 17 24 in.
 2 22½ in.
Four clay tile reducers, scrap wood, exterior paint, and stain.

FURNITURE
WITH
FLAIR

There's more to a deck or patio than wood and concrete. To make your "live-the-good-life" area even better, you need to furnish it with flair. And you can do just that with any of the projects in this chapter. Whether it's a picnic table, a bench, or a chaise you need, you'll find the projects presented here great-looking, yet practical.

These outdoor furniture pieces have a rustic look that helps them blend with their surroundings. And the design lines are simple, so all the projects are within the range of your capabilities.

Choose your project materials according to the use they'll get and the look you want. Make your selection from good-looking softwoods, such as redwood and cedar, and exterior-grade plywoods. Then use non-rusting hardware, exterior paint, and wood stain to ensure a long life for your projects.

Adapt the units' size, if you wish, but follow the basic dimensions for properly scaled furniture.

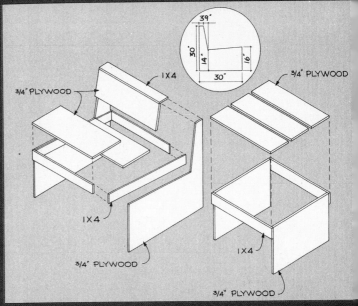

GO-TOGETHER-FAST TABLE AND CHAIRS

Attractive patio furniture can b[e] difficult to find. But if you buil[d] this project, you'll have furn[i]ture that's durable and good looking to boot. You can make these units in about the time i[t] would take to shop furniture stores, and you'll save some money, too. So, why not build one or a bunch for a patio ar[-]rangement that's hard to top!

1 Make a pattern for the chair's side panels (see sketch) and lay out on ¾-inch plywood.
2 Cut all of the plywood pieces for the table and chair (be sure to fig-ure the width of your saw blade when measuring).
3 Sand the edges of all of the ply-wood pieces and fill all exposed plywood edges with waterproof filler.
4 Cut 1x4s to length for the chair box, the top rail trim, and the table stretchers.
5 Assemble chair box with butt joints as shown on page 91, using waterproof glue and either finish-ing nails or screws.
6 Screw the plywood side pan-els to the box. Countersink the screws. Attach the two rails to the panels for the table in same man-ner as for chair.
7 Attach the plywood seat and back to the chair and top pieces t[o] the table, using wood screws. At[-]tach the 1x4 top rails to plywoo[d] panels in same manner.
8 Paint the side panels the desire[d] color. Stain the chair seat and back and tabletop. For a smooth surface, apply two coats of exte[-]rior varnish.

Materials (for table and chair):
1x4 redwood—16 ft.
  5 24 in.
  2 30 in.
¾-in. exterior plywood—1½ sht[s]
  2 22½x16 in.   1 9¼x24 in[.]
  3 7¼x24 in.   2 30x30 in.
  2 11¼x24 in.
Waterproof glue and filler, exterio[r]
paint, stain, and varnish[.]

REDWOOD CUBE FURNITURE

These little cubes can make the difference between a stand-up affair and a real sit-down garden party. Basically, they're plywood boxes covered with redwood 1x4s. They go together so quickly and easily that you can build them one weekend and entertain the next.

1 Lay out the pattern for the sides of the cube on a sheet of plywood, then cut the pieces. (Allow for the width of your saw blade.)

2 Assemble the four sides with butt joints (see page 91). Use glue and either nails or screws.

3 Cut a square for the top of the unit from ¾-inch plywood. Make sure that the edges of the plywood are flush with the outside faces of the plywood box. Glue and nail top to the box. Then, paint with exterior paint. Let dry. Prestain the 1x4s if desired.

4 Cut lengths of 1x4s long enough so you can miter corners for a picture frame effect around plywood box. Miter each piece of 1x4 as you go; apply top pieces first, then work down, using glue and nails. Position top 1x4 one inch above plywood top.

5 If you did not prestain, apply oil to 1x4s. For use as a seating cube, add a 16x16x4-inch cushion.

Materials (for one box):
1x4 redwood—18 ft.
    12 18 in.
¾-in. exterior plywood—1 sht.
    2 14½x16½ in.
    1 16½x16½ in.
    2 14½x15 in.
Waterproof glue, exterior paint, and weathering oil or stain.

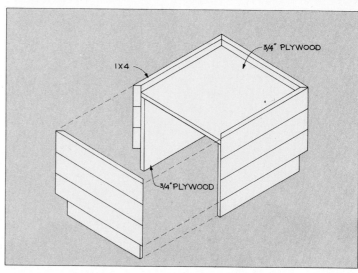

3/4" PLYWOOD

1X4

3/4" PLYWOOD

GO-ANYWHERE CANVAS SLINGS

Use these little canvas sling chairs beside the pool, at the lake, on the deck, or wherever you go. Designed to fold up, they're easy to pack in the trunk and carry under your arm. The frame and canvas cover are a snap to make. And, you can replace the sling with a new color whenever you like.

1 Cut canvas pieces. Turn under long sides on one piece ½ inch, twice, and stitch in place. Then make casing at ends of canvas to accommodate 1-inch dowels; wrap canvas around dowel, allowing two inches at back. Cut a slot in top casing at back to attach leg to dowel. Turn end raw edges under one inch, then stitch through three thicknesses of canvas. Set other canvas aside.

2 Cut two 1x4s at 40½ inches with 40 degree angle at bottom, and one at 27 inches with 20 degree angle at bottom. Cut top of shorter leg to receive dowel (see sketch).

3 Drill ⅜-inch holes halfway through the width of the 1x4 front legs in the two places indicated in sketch, then drill pilot holes to accommodate lag screws.

4 Cut dowels 24 inches long. Finish wood with two coats of urethane finish. Slip dowels through canvas sling. Then, with 6-inch screws, bolt uprights to dowels. Plug holes with ⅜-inch dowel.

5 Bolt back leg to top dowel with the 4-inch lag screws.

6 Drill two holes in each leg. Run cord through the holes as shown; adjust and tie off.

7 Make cushion from other piece of canvas and polyester fiberfill.

Materials (for one chair):
1x4 pine—10 ft.
  2 40½ in.   1 27 in.
Two 1-inch dowels 24 inches long, 10 feet ½-inch cord, four ⅜x6-inch lag screws and washers, two ⅜x4-inch lag screws and washers, two 26x48-inch pieces canvas; polyester fiberfill, and urethane finish.

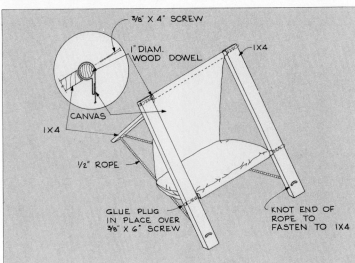

3/8" X 4" SCREW
1" DIAM. WOOD DOWEL
1X4
CANVAS
1X4
½" ROPE
GLUE PLUG IN PLACE OVER 3/8" X 6" SCREW
KNOT END OF ROPE TO FASTEN TO 1X4

TURN-AROUND, UP-OR-DOWN LATTICE CUBES

These tricky cubes can do almost anything you want them to. They work great for tables, stools, or potted plant stands. The lightweight construction makes the units quite easy to move and rearrange. And as a bonus, you can build the table for a handy, out-of-the-way place to store the cubes.

1 Plan the overall dimensions, then cut the frame of each box from 2x2s. Assemble frame with butt joints, using waterproof glue and finishing nails or screws. (For extra stability, you may want to use a metal angle and screws at each joint.)

2 Cut a flush bottom for each box from ¾-inch plywood. Scribe a circle large enough to hold a plant pot in the center of the plywood. Then drill a ½-inch hole at the inner edge of the circle to enable you to insert a saber saw blade. Cut out circles; sand and fill edges with waterproof filler. Attach bottom to frame using glue and finishing nails.

3 Cut lengths of lattice to cover five sides of each box. Attach strips to framework with finishing nails so they are flush with top and bottom of box.

4 Cut 2x2s for legs and top of table framework. The top should have four divisions the same size as the cubes that fit below. Assemble framework with butt joints, using glue and nails.

5 Cut lengths of lattice for tabletop to fit flush with the edge of the frame. Nail in place with finishing nails. Paint all surfaces with exterior paint.

Materials (for project shown):
2x2 redwood—96 ft.

4	38½ in.	1	37 in.
5	18 in.	16	15¾ in.
6	17¾ in.	32	15 in.

¾-in. exterior plywood—½ sht.
1½x⅜-inch lattice—288 ft.
   192 18 in.
Waterproof glue, filler, and exterior paint.

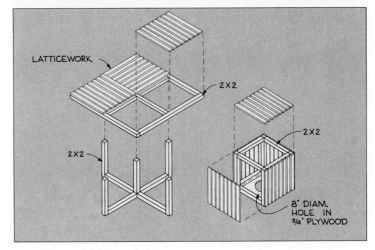

LATTICEWORK

2 X 2

2 X 2

2 X 2

8″ DIAM. HOLE IN ¾″ PLYWOOD

LATTICE POTTING/DISPLAY CABINET

A project as refreshing as it is functional, this unit will give you work space—plus. Use it for displaying your plants or storing potting materials.

1 Plan dimensions, making tabletop 36 inches high. Build framework for storage unit, table, and doors from 2x2s. Cut 1x1s to fit inside all framework except doors and tabletop so lattice is flush with frame. Butt-joint to 2x2s.

2 Cut out shelves, bottom, and back of lower section from ¾-inch plywood. Notch bottom and middle shelves to receive the 2x2s. Attach plywood to 2x2s.

3 Attach lattice to the 1x1 ledger at 45 degree angle. Attach lattice to doors and tabletop.

4 Drill 2x2 leg supports to receive bolts. Attach supports to tabletop with bolts.

5 Attach tabletop and doors to storage unit with butt hinges.

6 Finish with paint or stain. Attach door pulls and catches.

Materials (for project shown):
2x2 fir or redwood—88 ft.

4 72 in.	2 33 in.
6 33 in.	2 9 in.
6 12 in.	2 24 in.
2 36 in.	2 16 in.
4 13½ in.	1 6 in.
4 33 in.	

¾-in. exterior plywood—1 sht.

2 36x14 in.	1 36x36 in.
1 36x12 in.	

1½x¼-inch lattice—360 ft.
1x1 fir or redwood—60 ft.
Four bolts, washers, and wing nuts; three sets loose-pin butt hinges; two door pulls; two catches; glue; and paint or stain.

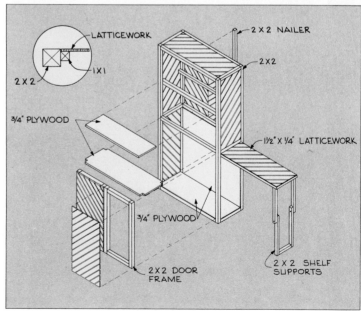

EASY-DOES-IT PLANTER/BENCH GROUPING

Talk about easy! This project almost builds itself. The rustic cedar planters go together in a flash, and the benches almost that quickly. But best of all, if you decide to move, you can knock these beauties apart and take them along. Make as few or as many as you want and arrange them to suit your taste.

1 For the planter, cut four equal lengths of 1x12. Then, measure 3 inches from each end of each board and cut a notch 5½ inches deep and ¾ inch wide.

2 Slip the sides together.

3 For the bench, cut the 1x4s for the supports, then glue and nail together using butt joints (see sketch).

4 To construct seat portion of bench, lay 10 of the 12 long 1x3s on edge side by side, making sure that their ends align.

5 Starting 2 inches in from each end, make a dado cut 2½ inches wide and ¾ inch deep in all of the boards. Make another dado cut midway between.

6 Center 1x3 blocks over the 1x4 cleats and nail together.

7 Spread adhesive over the 1x3 blocks, then position the dadoed 1x3s over the 1x3 blocks, with a spacer between each.

8 Position remaining 1x3s flush with edge of 1x4 cleats.

9 Drill pilot holes in each slot through 1x3 blocks and 1x4 cleats as shown. Secure bench top to uprights with adhesive and screws.

10 Treat bench and planter with stain or weathering oil.

Materials (for one planter and one 6-foot bench):

1x12 cedar—12 ft.
    4 36 in.

1x3 redwood—76 ft.
    12 72 in.   33 ½ in.
    3 13 in.

1x4 redwood—28 ft.
    3 14½ in.   6 13¼ in.
    6 14¾ in.   6 13 in.

Exterior adhesive, and stain or weathering oil.

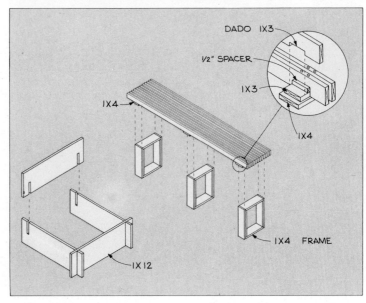

DADO 1X3
½" SPACER
1X3
1X4
1X4
1X4 FRAME
1X12

CONTEMPORARY PARK BENCHES

These updated versions of old park benches make eye-catching additions to any outdoor area. You'll want to make several to use on the patio, and possibly a few more for a rest area under a shady tree.

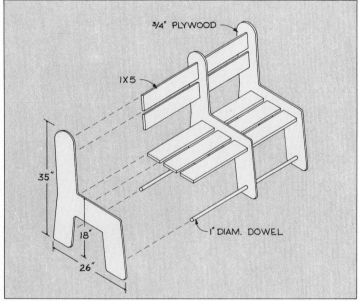

3/4" PLYWOOD

1X5

35"

18"

26"

1" DIAM. DOWEL

1 Lay out pattern for bench sides on ¾-inch plywood. (Use two sides for the single bench; three for the double bench.) Be sure to figure in the width of your saw blade when measuring. Cut out with a saber saw.

2 Cut slots in center bench support to accommodate 1x5 slats. Rout inside of end panels half the depth of the plywood to accommodate slats. Drill 1-inch-diameter holes in center support to accommodate 1-inch dowels; drill inside of end panels half the depth of the plywood.

3 Cut 1x5s to length for slats for backs and seats. Slide 1x5s and dowels through slots and holes in center support; glue with waterproof glue. Then attach 1x5s and dowels to end panels, using wa-

terproof glue and countersunk screws. For extra stability, attach ledger strips to middle and end panels; screw 1x5s to ledgers.

4 Fill all holes and exposed plywood edges with wood putty; sand units smooth.

5 Paint benches with primer-type sealer and finish with two coats of exterior-grade paint.

Materials (for one single and one double bench):

1x5 redwood—30 ft.
  5 42¼ in.
  5 21½ in.

1-inch wood dowel—12 ft.
  2 42¼ in.   2 21½ in.

¾-in. exterior plywood—1 sht.
Waterproof glue, wood putty, exterior primer, and paint.

LAZY-DAY CHAISE LOUNGE

Just imagine lying back and soaking up the sun on this handsome two-toned wood lounge. A simple construction of redwood 2x4s, it's the perfect project for poolside, patio, or backyard. You'll probably want to build more than one, since it's also great bench seating when a big crowd gathers.

1 Build the tall frame with 2x4s. Cut the 2x4 horizontal stretcher 15½ inches, the top rail 18½ inches, and the two verticals 25 inches. Miter vertical and horizontal pieces. Drill ¾-inch holes ¾ inch deep as shown in sketch, then screw frame together. Locate stretcher about halfway up uprights.

2 Build the lower frame, using 2x4s and a 1x4. Cut 2x4 horizontal stretcher and 1x4 top rail as for the tall frame. Cut miters in the 2x4s and the 1x4.

3 Assemble lower frame with screws set in ¾x¾-inch holes. Do not attach the 1x4.

4 Cut 2x4s to length for seat. Notch two outside 2x4s so they receive both tall and short legs. Then, cut into the five 2x4s the depth of the 1x4 so top rail will fit flush with seat.

5 Add long 2x4 stretcher between frames for stability.

6 Attach 2x4 seat to horizontal stretchers with screws. Drill ¼x¾-inch holes through 1x4 into 2x4s, then screw 1x4 in place.

7 Plug holes with ¾-inch dowel.

8 Sand units smooth. Finish with stain or weathering oil.

Materials (for project shown):
2x4 redwood—42 ft.

5 54 in.	1 18½ in.
1 35 in.	2 16 in.
2 15½ in.	2 25 in.

1x4 redwood—2 ft.

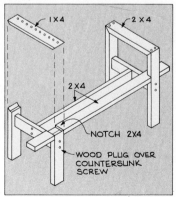

1 18½ in.
One 24-inch-long ¾-inch dowel, waterproof glue, and penetrating stain or weathering oil.

Labels in sketch: 1 X 4 · 2 X 4 · 2 X 4 · NOTCH 2X4 · WOOD PLUG OVER COUNTERSUNK SCREW

DESIGNER REDWOOD PICNIC TABLE

If you've always liked the flavor of outdoor eating, but loathed the inconvenience, here's your answer—the picnickers' picnic table. Designed as two benches and a table, and built with sturdy materials, it can withstand even the roughest use.

1 Construct benches first. Cut 2x4 uprights to length. Then cut horizontals and spacers for legs and bolt between uprights.

2 Build the 2x2 seats, allowing 1½ inches between each 2x2. Cut the framework first, mitering corners. Do not assemble. Cut additional 2x2s for the seat surface. Nail the two outside short 2x2s to longer frame.

3 Insert and nail long 2x2s for the seat to frame end and other 2x2s. Insert short 2x2s and nail through frame. Attach to crosspieces with nails.

4 Construct tabletop as you did the benches, but use 2x4 material for the frame and 2x2s for the table surface. Then construct 2x4 uprights (with mitered corners) to support tabletop.

5 Attach tabletop to uprights by nailing through frame to uprights. Nail the uprights to the bench horizontals. Nail a stretcher to bottom 2x4 of uprights. Nail bench seats to bench uprights.

6 Sand to smooth all surfaces. Finish wood with penetrating stain or weathering oil.

Materials (for project shown):
2x4 redwood—70 ft.

2	72 in.	8	25⅛ in.
2	30 in.	2	60 in.
4	28⅜ in.	8	16⅜ in.
4	17⅞ in.	4	3 in.

2x2 redwood—158 ft.

1	54 in.	4	14 in.
11	26¾ in.	22	10¾ in.
22	21⁹⁄₁₆ in.	16	21⁹⁄₁₆ in.
4	72 in.		

Eight 4¾-inch galvanized carriage bolts, waterproof glue, and stain or weathering oil.

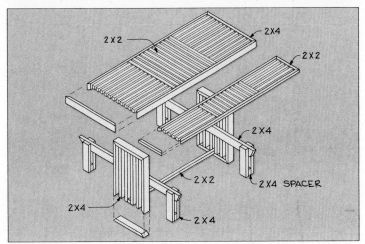

2 X 2
2 X 4
2 X 2
2 X 4
2 X 2
2 X 4 SPACER
2 X 4
2 X 4

PROJECTS
FOR
PLANT
LOVERS

Shrubs, trees, and blossoming plants of all shapes and colors will look even more appealing when complemented with the projects you'll find in this chapter. Spread across the next few pages is a wide array of planter boxes and arbors, and even a fence/screen with hidden shelves to show off your collection of green and flowering plants.

Feel free to mix and match several of these projects, and to use them as the final touch for a landscape or decorating scheme in need of that certain something extra.

You can build them exactly as shown, or easily adapt sizes, shapes, and textures to your own particular needs.

Or, use these plans as a springboard to design your own planter and fence arrangements. The possibilities are almost endless, and we guarantee—your dull entry or monotonous deck will never be the same.

A-FRAMED ARBOR

The simplicity of A-frame construction makes this garden archway an easy—and spectacular—landscape addition. The clean, triangular unit draped with fruitful grape vines or colorful flowering creepers is guaranteed to add flair to your garden entry or brighten a dull corner. And, you can build this magnificent structure in less than a day.

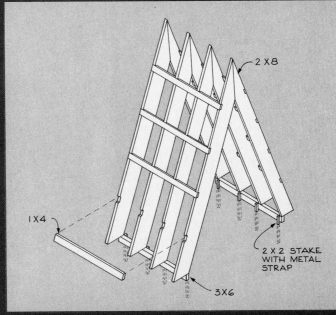

2 X 8

1 X 4

2 X 2 STAKE WITH METAL STRAP

3 X 6

1 Draw a 90° L on a drive. (Make the base 2 feet 8 inches long and the upright 12 feet long.)
2 Measure a 12-foot diagonal from the end of the base and mark its intersection on the upright.
3 Lay one of the 2x8s between these points and mark the mitered ends according to the 90° L, then divide the long edge of the 2x8 into five equal parts. Over each division mark, center a ¾x3½-inch notch (see sketch). Cut and use this piece as a pattern for all the 2x8s.
4 Assemble the A-shaped supports (see sketch) with large nails through the points and use smaller nails to toenail the sides.
5 Stand the A-shaped frames upright, attaching the 1x4s to each

side as you do (see sketch). Fasten with nails.
6 Toenail the penta-treated 3x6 bases along the bottom of each side with nails (see sketch).
7 Position structure and drive stakes as shown, then attach them to the 3x6s with straps.
8 Apply stain or oil.

Materials (for project shown):
2x8 redwood—96 ft.
  8 12 ft.
2x2 redwood—12 ft.
  8 18 in.
1x4 redwood—32 ft.
  8 48 in.
3x6 redwood—8 ft.
  2 48 in.
Eight 8-inch metal straps, penta, and weathering oil or stain.

TRAPEZOIDAL PLANTERS

Add interest to your floral groupings with these handsome natural wood containers. They'll make your best arrangements look even better.

1 Cut out a cardboard trapezoid side pattern. (Height is 11 inches. Width may be up to two feet; bottom width should be 3 inches less.)

2 Cut four 1x8s and four 1x4s to length of pattern's top width.

3 Build each of the four sides by fastening the edges of the two boards together with corrugated fasteners (see sketch).

4 Trace the cardboard pattern on each set of side boards and cut out with a circular saw. (NOTE: Use the saw's 45° setting to cut sloping vertical edge. To reduce splitting, score the tracing lines with a utility knife and cut to the outside of the score.)

5 Glue the sides together and fasten with nails.

6 Cut the plywood bottom to size and nail to the sides.

7 Attach 1x4 footpads with nails; or, for more mobility, use casters.

8 Drill ½-inch drain holes and soak inside with penta. (NOTE: Allow penta to dry two to three days before using planter.)

9 Treat outside of planter with stain or weathering oil.

Materials (for each planter shown):
1x4 redwood—8 ft.
1x8 redwood—8 ft.
¾-in. ext. plywood—24-in. square
Penta, stain or weathering oil, exterior adhesive, and four plate-type casters (optional).

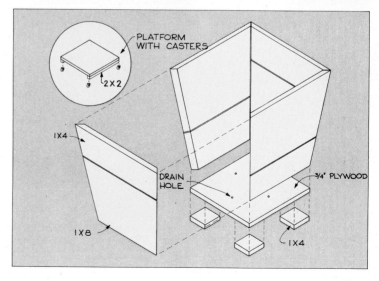

PLATFORM WITH CASTERS

2X2

1X4

DRAIN HOLE

¾" PLYWOOD

1X8

1X4

PLANT DISPLAY / PRIVACY FENCE

Pots full of your favorite greenery turn this ordinary privacy fence into a lush display.

1 Set the 4x6 post as instructed on page 88. (NOTE: To determine the span—not over 8 feet—start with a 1-inch space, then add 2½ inches for each 2x2 and 4½ inches for each 2x4.)

2 Mark and cut post 8½ feet high.

3 On back of the post, measure down one foot and cut a full-width notch 1½ inches deep and 5½ inches long. Cut two other notches farther down the post.

4 Level a line from post top and mark its intersection on an existing wall or building. Cut an identically notched 2x6 to go from that point to the ground and nail it to the wall.

5 Fit and nail 2x6 crossmembers.

6 Tie a string between the post and wall plate, 1½ inches from their tops. Then, using 1-inch lumber as a spacer, nail on the slats. Keep slats flush with string and 1½ inches from ground.

7 Cut a 2x6 cap and nail to tops of the slats.

8 Paint or stain all fence parts.

Materials (for screen 8½ feet high and 7½ feet long):

4x6 redwood or cedar
   1 10 ft. 6 in. (min.)
2x2 redwood or cedar—110 ft.
  11 100 in.
2x4 redwood or cedar—120 ft.
  12 100 in.
2x6 redwood or cedar—42 ft.
   3 93 in.
   1 88 in.
   1 8 ft. 6 in.

Penta, and stain or paint.

CONTEMPORARY CUBIST PLANTER

This dramatic planter makes bold use of contrasting white and raised dark lines in the form of a classic cube. The clean, stark simplicity of this outdoor structure will enhance your green and flowering vegetation alike. Whether used to conceal a pot, as shown here, or filled with dirt to plant in directly, this unit gives your landscape a modern flair.

1 Assemble the plywood box, as shown in sketch, using exterior glue and nails. Of course, use exterior grade plywood.

2 Paint the exterior of box with white house paint as per manufacturer's instructions.

3 Drill ½-inch drain holes in the bottom and liberally coat the inside with penta preservative. (NOTE: Allow penta to dry two to three days before using planter.)

4 Rip eight of the 24-inch 1x3s with a 45° bevel along one edge to make mitered corners (see sketch).

5 Miter four 20-inch 1x4s to form the base. Glue and nail together. Center base on bottom of box and attach with nails.

6 To build the planter's top frame, miter the corners of the 26½-inch 1x4s and fasten together on the bottom side with corrugated fasteners and exterior glue.

7 Stain all of the slats, the top frame, and the 1x4 base.

8 Center the top frame on the box, then attach with glue and finishing nails.

9 Evenly space six slats on each side and glue and nail in place.

Materials (for a 2-foot-square planter):

1x3 redwood—58 ft.
    4 26½ in.
  24 24 in.

1x4 redwood—8 ft.
    4 20 in.

¾-in. exterior plywood—1 sheet
  2 23¼ x 22¾ in.
  2 23¼ x 24 in.
  1 24x24 in.

Exterior glue, primer, white house paint, stain, and penta.

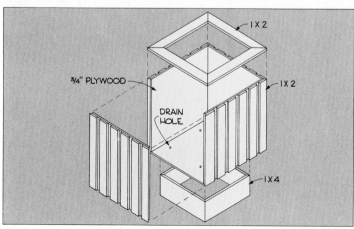

1 X 2

1 X 2

¾" PLYWOOD

DRAIN HOLE

1 X 4

LONG-AND-LOW PLANTER BOX

This stylish planter/pot tray leads a double life. It's a great summer show-off spot for your potted house plants. Just bring them outside and arrange them in the planter. Or, by treating the unit with penta and adding layers of gravel and dirt, it becomes a roomy planter box. Either way, this contemporary design is sure to complement your yard.

1 Determine the desired length of your planter box and cut the 2x6 side pieces.

2 Cut the 1x12 bottom and the 1x2 nailers 3 inches shorter than 2x6 sides (see sketch).

3 Measure the exact width of the 1x12 (approximately 11½ inches) and cut two ends to match. (NOTE: This step is necessary because lumber varies up to ¼ inch from standard width.)

4 Attach nailers flush with the bottom of the 2x6 sides and 1½ inches short of each end (nail in a zigzag pattern every 4 inches).

5 Nail the bottom to the nailers, keeping the 1x12 flush with the ends of the nailers.

6 Nail sides and ends together as shown in sketch, leaving the ends 1 inch lower than the sides. The ends form legs to raise the main body off the ground, allowing for freer drainage.

7 Drill ½-inch drain holes in bottom and treat inside heavily with penta. (NOTE: Allow penta to dry two to three days before using planter.) Treat outside with stain or weathering oil.

8 If you'll use the planter on the ground, set it in a bed of pea gravel.

Materials (for one 5-foot-long planter):
2x6 redwood—12 ft.
  2 60 in.
  2 11½ in.
1x2 redwood—10 ft.
  2 57 in.
1x12 redwood—6 ft.
  1 57 in.
Penta, and stain or weathering oil or paint.

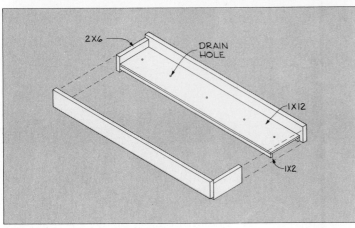

2X6

DRAIN HOLE

1X12

1X2

RUSTIC PLANTER MODULES

If your deck took over valuable garden space when it went in, here's your chance to get some of it back. By stacking these planter modules in ascending tiers, you can create the illusion of large garden space with just a few square feet of plantable dirt. So indulge your green thumb. Spruce up that unused corner of your deck with these cedar stackables.

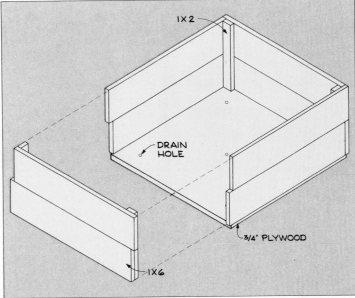

1 Cut eight rough cedar 1x6 side pieces ½ inch shorter than the sides of the square bottom.

2 Build the planter sides in two sections, both made with four pieces nailed together. Each 1x6 is butt-jointed at one end and lap-jointed at the other (see sketch).

3 Stack the two side sections with like joints opposite each other (see sketch) and attach by nailing a 1x2 cleat in each corner.

4 Cut the square plywood bottom and drill ½-inch holes for drainage and ventilation (see sketch). (NOTE: When stacking several of these modules, omit bottoms in all but the top unit.)

5 Nail the bottom to the sides of the planter box. (NOTE: Remember to center bottom, since it's smaller than the sides.)

6 On modules with bottoms that sit directly on the deck, use 1x4 rough cedar squares as foot pads.

7 Liberally coat the inside of planter with penta. (NOTE: Allow penta to dry two to three days before using planter.) Treat exterior with weathering oil.

8 Penta-treat the deck under planter modules to hinder rot.

Materials (for a 2-foot-square module):
1x2 rough cedar—4 ft.
    4 11 in.
1x6 rough cedar—16 ft.
    8 23½ in.
¾-in. exterior plywood—
¼ sheet
    1 24x24 in.
Penta and weathering oil.

"LAYER CAKE" REDWOOD PLANTERS

Sturdy and visually striking, these redwood planters are just the thing to show off a favorite collection of flowers. The interlocking "fingers" that make up the tiered sides give these units the strength and detail that make them something special. The perfect way to perk up a dreary entry or desolate deck, these planters are well worth your building effort.

1 Cut a piece of ¾-inch plywood the desired size for the square bottom of your planter.

2 To ensure good ventilation and drainage, cut four redwood foot pads and fasten to the bottom with exterior glue and nails.

3 Drill five ½-inch drain holes in the plywood bottom.

4 To make the five-tiered sides, cut 10 redwood 2x2s the length of a bottom side and 10 more 3 inches shorter than that length.

5 Attach a long 2x2 to opposite sides of the bottom. Drive nails through the plywood into the 2x2s.

6 Along the other two edges of the square bottom, attach two of the shorter 2x2s flush with the ends and between the two longer 2x2s (see sketch).

7 Attach each succeeding row of 2x2s so that a long piece laps over the ends of two long pieces in the row below. Fasten these rows of 2x2s by drilling pilot holes, then nailing.

8 Heavily treat the inside and bottom of the planter with penta, and apply stain or weathering oil to the outside of the structure. (NOTE: Allow penta to dry two to three days before using planter.)

Materials (for a 2-foot-square planter):
2x2 redwood—40 ft.
   10 24 in.
   10 21 in.
1x4 redwood—2 ft.
   4 3½ in.
¾-in. exterior plywood—
¼ sheet
   1 24x24 in.
Penta and weathering oil.

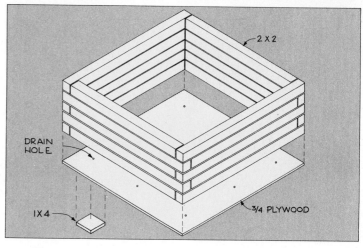

2 X 2

DRAIN HOLE

1 X 4

¾ PLYWOOD

FLOWER TROUGHS

These sleek, stylish planter boxes are a "can't miss" project for trimming the edges of your patio or deck. Made of redwood for long-lasting beauty, they adapt easily to a number of planting arrangements. The planters shown are six feet long, but you may want to vary the dimensions or even make more than one to solve a special landscaping problem.

1 Cut six 1x6 redwood pieces for the sides. (NOTE: Length over 6 feet requires three leg assemblies.)

2 From plywood, cut the bottom to the same length as the sides.

3 Cut six redwood 1x6 end pieces 14 inches long.

4 To make the two U-shaped legs, nail or screw two 22-inch 2x6 uprights on each side of both ends of a 2x6 bottom support that is 11 inches wider than the planter box (see sketch).

5 Build the planter in three sections. To construct the bottom, nail two sides to the edge of the bottom flush at the ends and butted into the side pieces (see sketch). The second and third sections go together with simple butt joints.

6 Fasten the three layers together with corrugated fasteners.

7 Position the leg assemblies approximately 12 inches from the end of the planter and nail on.

8 Drill ½-inch drain holes in the bottom and treat the inside with penta. (NOTE: Allow penta to dry two to three days before using planter.)

9 Stain entire unit.

Materials (for a 6-foot-long planter box):

1x6 redwood—44 ft.
  6 72 in.
  6 14 in.

2x6 redwood—22 ft.
  8 22 in.
  2 25½ in.

¾-in. exterior plywood—½ sheet
  1 12½x72 in.

Corrugated fasteners, penta, and stain or weathering oil.

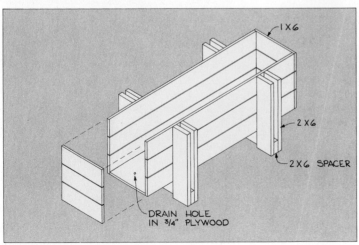

1X6

2X6

2X6 SPACER

DRAIN HOLE IN ¾" PLYWOOD

BUILT-IN PLANTER AND FOUNTAIN

Don't let a plain garage or house wall stand in the way of your landscaping plans. Transform it with this spectacular planter and fountain. Those monotonous walls will become neutral backdrops for this striking display of shrubs, trees, and flowers. The irregular angles of the planter box counterpoint the fountain's gentle curves.

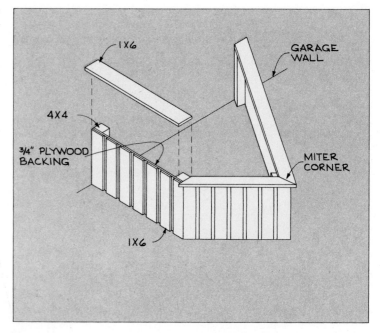

1 Decide on a good location for the planter and stake out the planter's outline to determine spacing of the posts. (NOTE: In planning the length of the three walls, add 5½ inches for the first vertical wall slat and 6½ inches for each succeeding slat.

2 Set the four factory penta-treated or redwood posts in concrete as described on page 88. Be sure that they are plumb and that the distance between the points where the wall sections join complies with step 1.

3 Determine planter height and level a line from post to post. Cut each post to that height.

4 Cut ¾-inch plywood to height and length for each panel.

5 Prime and paint the outside surfaces of each panel with several coats of black or dark brown exterior house paint.

6 Heavily coat panel edges and backs with penta. (NOTE: Be sure to allow penta to dry two to three days before using the planter. Otherwise, your plants may sustain damage.)

7 Cut the required number of 1x6 redwood vertical slats the same height as the planter panels.

8 Temporarily tack the plywood panels in place. Then determine the angle of each corner panel with a bevel square and rip scrap 1x6 to test those angles. Make any adjustments necessary to ensure a good fit, then rip slats to use on the corners and against the garage.

9 Take the panels off the posts and nail the 1x6 verticals to the painted surface. Make sure that the 1x6s are flush with the top of the plywood. Do not attach the beveled pieces.

10 Install each of the fence panels flush with the top of the posts with nails.

11 Fit the beveled corner pieces. (NOTE: This takes up any inconsistency of fit and makes for a neat job.) Attach to the plywood with nails, then toenail into each other along the edges.

12 Miter the 2x6 top caps to fit centered over the walls. Fasten to the posts with nails, then into the plywood and toenail the ends of the caps together at the joints with more nails.

13 Stain the 1x6s and the 2x6s, or treat with weathering oil.

14 Install the precast concrete fountain and submersible pump as per manufacturer's instructions and local code.

Materials:

4x4 redwood
Enough to go from top of planter wall into the ground below the frost line. If desired, substitute factory-treated posts for the redwood.

1x6 redwood
Enough to form fence verticals.

¾-in. exterior plywood
Enough to serve as backing for the 1x6 redwood.

2x6 redwood
Enough to make fence cap. Exterior primer paint, black or dark brown paint, stain or weathering oil, penta, precast concrete fountain, and submersible pump.

STEP-AND-PLANTER ENTRY

This easily built step-and-planter unit does much more than just beautify your entry. It makes for a sleek, practical transition from patio to house, and it's easily adjusted to match the height of your door.

Your planters, like the ones shown here overflowing with colorful geraniums, will give your family and friends a cheerful welcome.

1 To build the step, drill three ⅜-inch holes in one of the 72-inch 2x4s. Drill them 10 inches from each end and in the center. Use this piece as a pattern for drilling the rest of the 2x4s.
2 Over the three ⅜-inch holes in the two outside 2x4s, drill ½-inch-deep holes the diameter of the washers to countersink nuts.
3 Thread a nut and washer on one end of each rod and fit through 2x4s. Use four flat washers for spacers between each. Thread nuts on other end.
4 Fasten 1x4 step supports (flush front and back) with nails.
5 Using butt joints, build a 2x4 planter base the same width as the step and 30 inches long (see sketch). Fasten with nails.
6 Build the 2x6 redwood planter as you did the 2x4 base, but add a ¾-inch plywood bottom.
7 Drill ½-inch drain holes in the bottom and treat inside of planter with a heavy coat of penta. (NOTE: Allow penta to dry two to three days before using planter.)
8 Apply stain or weathering oil.
9 Set in gravel for drainage.

Materials (for one 72x14-inch step and two 30x14-inch boxes):
2x4 redwood—62 ft.
  8 72 in.   4 11 in.
  4 30 in.
1x4 redwood—6 ft.
  4 14 in.
2x6 redwood—14 ft.
  4 30 in.   4 11 in.
¾-in. exterior plywood—½ sht.
  2 30x14 in.
Three ⅜x14-inch threaded rods, 6 nuts and 90 flat washers, penta, and stain or weathering oil.

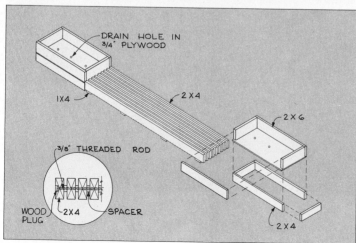

DRAIN HOLE IN ¾" PLYWOOD

1X4

2 X 4

2 X 6

⅜" THREADED ROD

WOOD PLUG

2X4

SPACER

2 X 4

HIDEWAY PLANTER/ PRIVACY FENCE

There's no reason to replace an undesirable view with a dull one. This privacy fence features a built-in view of its own—your favorite green and flowering plants. Rows of shelves with pot screens let you expand your garden and block out a parking area or your neighbor's yard, doing both in style.

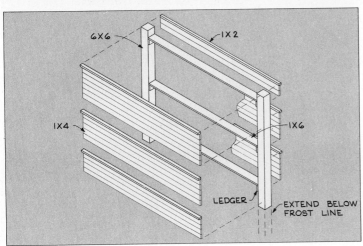

1 Set the 6x6 posts as directed on page 88. Make sure they are plumb, equidistant, and in a straight line with each other.

2 Determine fence height, using a line level, and cut off posts at that height.

3 Cover the back of the fence with redwood 1x4s starting flush with the top and working down. Do not splice all boards on the same post. Stagger the joints between posts using various lengths of 1x4.

4 Attach a 1x6 shelf between the posts and flush with the bottom of the top 1x4. Toenail the 1x6 to the posts and nail shelf to 1x4.

5 Evenly space the two lower shelves below the top shelf. They must be flush with the bottom of one of the 1x4s on the back side (see sketch). Fasten as in step 4.

6 To form pot screens, nail one 1x4 to each shelf so the bottom edge is flush with the bottom of the shelf (see sketch).

7 Cover the front of the fence with redwood 1x4s (see sketch), and leave 10½ inches between the pot screen and the next group of 1x4s above it.

8 Nail 1x2 caps to the top edge of the 1x4 pot screen.

9 Coat the entire structure with stain or weathering oil.

Materials (for a 24-foot fence):
6x6 redwood—32 ft. (min.)
   4 96 in. (min.)
1x2 redwood—144 ft.
   18 96 in.
1x6 redwood—72 ft.
   9 90½ in.
1x4 redwood—720 ft.
Penta, and weathering oil or stain.

SUN SCREEN/ GRAPE ARBOR

Add another dimension to your garden with this natural redwood sun screen/arbor. It creates a striking backyard entrance or a spot of shade for a deck or patio. The massive 2x6 trellis is an attention grabber. At the same time, it makes an ideal frame for an arrangement of permanent and potted plants, shrubs, or trees.

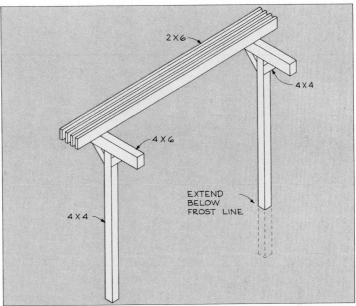

1 Set the 4x4 posts as described on page 88. Make sure they are parallel with each other and that the distance between them is four feet less than the length of the trellis rails. (NOTE: Use penta-treated or soaked posts.)

2 Level a line between the posts at a height of 6 to 6½ feet, and cut them off at that height.

3 Center the 4x6 crossmembers over the posts and toenail to the posts. (To determine the length of crossmembers, add 1½ inches for the first trellis rail and 5 inches for each rail thereafter. For example, ten rails would be 1½ plus 45 inches.)

4 Cut the diagonal 4x4 support members and nail in position.

5 Toenail the first 2x6 rail flush with the end of the 4x6 and extending past each crossmember.

6 Toenail each succeeding rail in position, leaving a 3½-inch space between them.

7 To keep the rails from twisting, you may want to block between them with 5-inch-long 2x4s. Install them flush with the top of the rails to leave space for drainage.

8 Treat all parts with penta or weathering oil.

Materials (for a 10-foot-long fence):

4x4 redwood—26 feet
   2 10 ft.
   4 14 in.

4x6 redwood—8 ft.
   2 46½ in.

2x6 redwood—100 ft.
   10 10 ft.

Penta and weathering oil.

RANDOM PLANTER COLUMN

If you're looking for an idea to turn on your deck, patio, or entry, try this beflowered planter column. This slender pillar is a decorative oasis in even the most uninspiring landscape. The tiny planters are just right for small vines or brightly flowered plants. And—best of all—your home can be better looking for this project in the space of a weekend.

1 Cut a 5½x3-inch notch in each end of the 4-foot 1x6s.

2 In the center of each of the four 14-inch 1x6 crossmembers cut a notch 1½ inches wide and 2¾ inches deep. (NOTE: Make sure both sets of two 14-inch pieces dovetail snugly and are flush with each other.) Fit crossmembers together and toenail at top and bottom using exterior glue.

3 Toenail the crossmember assemblies to the uprights (see sketch).

4 Build four simple butt-jointed planter boxes from redwood or cedar. Attach these to uprights at random heights with screws.

5 Drill ½-inch drain holes in the bottom of each planter.

6 Treat structure with penta and stain. (NOTE: Allow penta to dry two to three days before using planter.)

Materials (for a 4-foot unit):
1x6 redwood or cedar—34 ft.
   4 48 in.
   4 14 in.
   8 8 in.
   8 5½ in.
   4 6½ in.
Penta, stain, and wood screws.

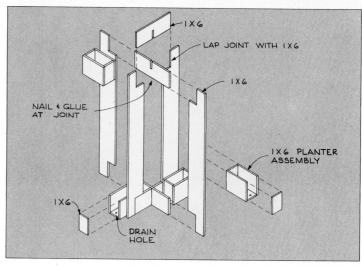

1X6

LAP JOINT WITH 1X6

1X6

NAIL & GLUE AT JOINT

1X6 PLANTER ASSEMBLY

1X6

DRAIN HOLE

GUARD RAIL PLANTERS

If you have a wall of glass in an area where someone might walk into it, protect your family and friends with this grouping of redwood planters. They solve your protection problem while adding a burst of color to cheer up a somber weathered deck. The planters shown here can also serve as a railing around a deck cutout for a basement window well.

1 Cut six 2x4s to length for the sides. (NOTE: Instructions apply to all three planters.)

2 On a flat surface lay three 2x4 side pieces tight against each other and flush at the ends. Fasten together with corrugated fasteners or, as an alternate method, nail on 10½-inch-long 1x2 cleats, 1½ inches in from the ends of the 2x4s.

3 Cut six 2x4s one foot long to form the ends. Fasten together in the center with corrugated fasteners or a 10½-inch 1x2 cleat.

4 Nail end panels between sides.

5 Cut bottoms for the planter boxes from ¾-inch plywood. Each bottom is the same length as the outside measurement of the planter but 1 inch narrower. Attach to the 2x4s with nails.

6 Add foot pads to the corners to aid drainage.

7 Drill ½-inch drain holes in bottom and coat the inside with penta. (NOTE: Allow penta to dry two to three days before using planter.)

8 Coat entire structure with stain or weathering oil.

Materials (for the three planters shown):

1x4 redwood—4 ft.
  12 3½ in.
2x4 redwood—96 ft.
  6 96 in.
  6 24 in.
  6 36 in.
  18 12 in.
¾-in. exterior plywood—1 sheet
  1 14x96 in.
  1 14x24 in.
  1 14x36 in.
Penta, stain or weathering oil, and corrugated fasteners.

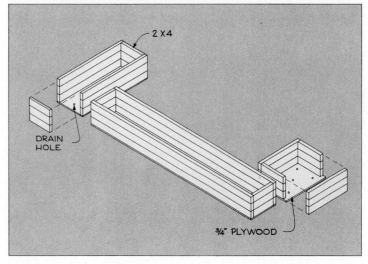

2 X 4

DRAIN HOLE

¾" PLYWOOD

SHADY PLACES

Fresh air, cool breezes, and sunshine are the joys of outdoor living areas. But even sun worshipers sometimes want to avoid all that glare. If that's your objective, spend a weekend constructing one of the sun screens presented in this section.

If simplicity of design and construction appeals to you, choose one of the two canvas-roofed projects. The freestanding unit at right is great for protecting a patio dining area. The other canvas project is supported by a trellis that's perfect for climbing plants.

You'll also find an easy-to-construct T-post porch roof that attaches to a garage, house, or storage shed. And, for the more ambitious, there are plans for an attractive arched roof that stands free or attaches to an existing structure, and a gazebo-type hut complete with benches.

So whether you want just a shady spot in your backyard or a stylish way to protect a patio, porch, or outdoor eating area, you're sure to find it here.

CANVAS-DRAPED SUN SCREEN

The words "simple" and "attractive" perfectly describe this patio sun roof. A sturdy redwood framework supports the airy, yet protective "ceiling" of canvas strips looped over 1x2s.

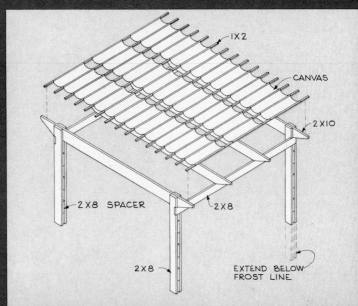

1X2

CANVAS

2X10

2X8 SPACER

2X8

2X8

EXTEND BELOW FROST LINE

1 Build posts as shown in sketch, using two 2x8s and three spacers for each post.

2 Make a mark 1½ feet from each end of all 2x10s. Make another mark two inches down from other side. Connect marks; saw angle.

3 Position outside two 2x10 rails as shown in sketch. Bolt rails.

4 Dado 2x8 supports just under angled end of outside rails to accommodate 2x8 crossmembers.

5 Treat posts with penta and set in concrete as directed on page 88. (Set posts 12 feet apart, measuring from outside corners of posts.)

6 Nail crossmembers to uprights.

7 Position the remaining 2x10 rails as shown. Toenail to 2x8s.

8 Stain framework and all 1x2s.

9 To attach middle canvas, position one canvas piece in center of a 1x2; nail. Measure 1½ feet of canvas; center on another 1x2. Nail. Repeat with remaining 1x2s.

10 Position remaining canvas pieces 10½ inches from either side of center strip; secure.

11 Hoist roof and let rest on the framework. Center over frame and position 1x2s at one-foot intervals, starting six inches from one end. Nail in place.

Materials (for project shown):
2x8 redwood or cedar—132 ft.
   8 11 ft. 6 in.   2 12 ft.
  12 12 in.
2x10 redwood or cedar—64 ft.
   4 15 ft.
1x2 redwood or cedar—180 ft.
  15 12 ft.
Three 3x21-foot pieces of light canvas, penta, and stain.

TRELLIS SUN ROOF

Looking for an idea that will make your patio even more of a crowd pleaser? This sun roof will do the trick, and it's easy to build. What's more, when Old Man Winter comes knocking, you can disassemble the roof and store it inside.

1 To assemble trellis frame, nail one 2x4 post at each end of the 2x4 top piece. Center remaining 2x4 post; nail. Position a 2x4 crossmember on each side of the center post one foot down from top piece; nail. Position remaining 2x4 crossmembers so they will be about two feet off the ground when trellis is erected; nail.

2 Drill holes to accommodate conduit in each 4x4 block, one foot from top of each outer post, and at top of the center post.

3 Treat posts with penta and set in concrete as directed on page 88. (Position just under 10 feet from existing structure.)

4 To complete trellis, position lath in chevron design as shown, cutting and mitering ends to fit. Glue and nail lath.

5 Stain or paint all wood.

6 Sew a 1½-inch casing on each long side of canvas piece. Slip conduit through each casing.

7 To attach roof, insert remaining conduit in hole in center post of trellis. Insert other end in 4x4 block. Bolt block to existing structure. Lay canvas over this conduit. Attach remaining conduits to trellis and house as above.

Materials (for project shown):
2x4 redwood—54 ft.
    3 12 ft.   4 33¾ in.
    1 72 in.
4x4 redwood—1 ft.
    3 4 in.
Redwood lath—80 ft.
One 7x10-foot piece canvas, three 10-foot pieces 1-inch aluminum conduit, penta preservative, and stain or exterior paint.

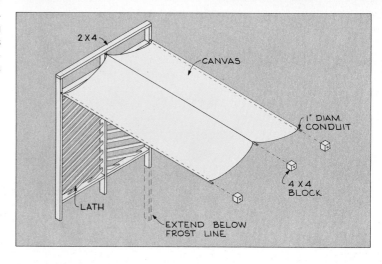

2 X 4

CANVAS

1" DIAM. CONDUIT

4 X 4 BLOCK

LATH

EXTEND BELOW FROST LINE

T-POST PORCH SHADE

This simple sun screen is the perfect complement to a small redwood deck or porch—and it's a snap to build. The clean, contemporary lines are a plus in any landscape, and you'll enjoy the interesting patterns of sunlight that filter through the slat roof.

1 Build the two supports as shown in the sketch. Be sure to center the crossmembers and position them 5½ inches from the top of the posts. Position spacers 12 inches from ends of 2x4s, and bolt members together.

2 Treat posts with penta and set in concrete as directed on page 88. (Space posts about nine feet apart and three feet from house.)

3 To stabilize structure, fasten strap to the house and to the ends of the crosspieces.

4 Nail a 2x4 to bottom of each side of each post as shown.

5 Position 1x6s as shown. Nail to spacers and posts.

6 For roof, start three inches from end and alternate 96- and 84-inch 1x2s at 1½-inch intervals. Nail to secure.

7 Apply stain or weathering oil.

Materials (for project shown):
1x2 redwood—354 ft.
   24 96 in.   23 84 in.
1x6 redwood—72 ft.
   6 12 ft.
2x4 redwood—56 ft.
   4 72 in.   8 27 in.
   4 24 in.
4x4 redwood—28 ft.
   4 9 in.   2 12 ft.
Two metal straps, penta, and stain or weathering oil.

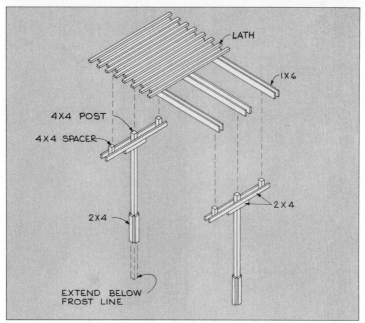

LATH
1X6
4X4 POST
4X4 SPACER
2X4
2X4
EXTEND BELOW FROST LINE

ARCHED PATIO ROOF

Attach this gently curved patio roof to your house, garage, or storage shed as directed below, or make it freestanding with support posts on both sides. Either way, it's a striking addition to your landscape.

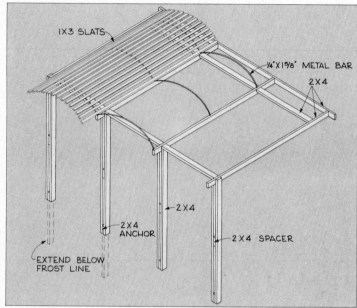

1X3 SLATS

¼" X 1⅝" METAL BAR

2 X 4

2 X 4

2 X 4 ANCHOR

2 X 4 SPACER

EXTEND BELOW FROST LINE

1 Bend each metal bar into curve, with a one-inch tab at each end. (Distance between ends of curve is 44 inches.)

2 Treat anchors with penta and set in concrete as directed on page 88. (Position anchors 44 inches apart and 7½ feet from existing structure.)

3 For each post, nail a spacer in center of a 2x4 upright. Align a second 2x4; nail.

4 Trim 1½ inches from top of all but outer two 2x4s as shown.

5 Bolt posts to anchors.

6 Nail 2x4 crosspieces as shown.

7 For back rail, bolt and nail a 2x4 to existing structure, aligning with end posts.

8 To build roof framework, nail the long 2x4s to the uprights and toenail to the back rail.

9 Nail remaining crosspieces 12 inches from back rail.

10 For each roof arch, use 16 slats and three curved metal bars. Position a bar in center and 12 inches from each end of slats. Space slats at one-inch intervals. Drill holes through bar and slats; bolt slats in place.

11 Drill holes in tabs of arches; bolt to framework.

12 Apply stain.

Materials (for project shown):
2x4 redwood—150 ft.

8 84 in.	4 6 in.
4 8 ft. 6 in.	4 48 in.
1 12 ft. 6 in.	6 44 in.

1x3 redwood slats—480 ft.
48 9 ft. 6 in.
Nine ¼x1⅝-inch metal bars 56 inches long, penta, and stain.

COME-RAIN COME-SHINE SHELTER

The possibilities for using this cozy shelter are almost limitless. It's a perfect retreat for warm-weather breakfasts and lunches, afternoon siestas, or just plain relaxing. Not only that, it's a great buy, considering the relatively small cost of the materials you'll need to build this attractive hut.

1 Make heavy paper patterns for pieces A, B, C, D, and E according to dimensions detailed below. Mark four each of pieces A, B, C, and D, and two of piece E on plywood sheets; cut out.
2 Position piece A on piece B, overlapping at top as shown; glue and nail. Repeat with remaining A and B pieces, making two right-hand sides and two left-hand sides.
3 For front framework, butt together the 6-inch edges of two B pieces at center front. Measure and cut a plywood gusset to fit over this seam. Glue and nail plywood gusset in place on inside, making sure B pieces butt together tightly. Repeat for back framework.
4 To attach front framework to back framework, position the 43½-inch 2x4 at gussets as shown. Glue and nail to both front and back gussets and plywood framework. Glue and nail a 45-inch 2x4 at each top corner and a 46½-inch 2x4 at bottom of each side as shown. On each side, glue and nail a 46½-inch 1x4 to front and back supports, with top edge 15½ inches from the ground.
5 For each bench, position one C piece inside front and another C piece inside back, fitting pieces over the 2x4 and butting up against the 1x4. Glue and nail C pieces to 2x4, 1x4, and plywood front or back. Add one E piece for bench front and two D pieces on bench sides as shown. (D pieces extend above top ¾ inch and fit against edge of A piece.) Glue and nail. Make bench top with 1x2s as shown in the sketch, glu-

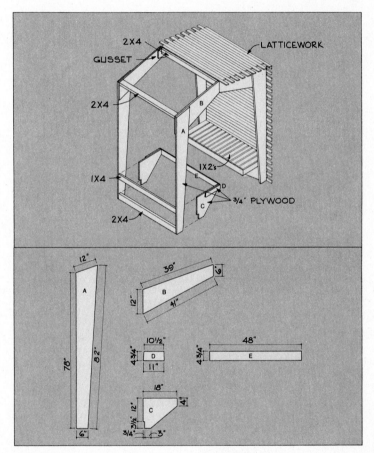

ing and nailing to secure.
6 Paint framework and benches.
7 Glue and nail redwood lath or latticework in place as shown, alternating overhang from front to back.
8 Apply stain or weathering oil to lath or latticework.

Materials (for project shown):
1x2 fir—108 ft.
　64 18¾ in.
1x4 fir—8 ft.
　2 46½ in.
2x4 fir—20 ft.
　2 45 in.
　2 46½ in.
　1 43½ in.
Redwood lath or 1½-in. lattice-work—702 ft.
　156 54 in.
¾-in. exterior plywood—2 shts.
Exterior glue, exterior paint, and stain or weathering oil.

CHILDREN'S PLAYTHINGS

Every child deserves a piece of the backyard to call his own. And, given a ladder to climb, a rope to swing on, or a beam to straddle, children can turn a simple framework of posts, boards, and plywood into imaginative arenas of never-ending fun.

You'll have fun, too, when you build the projects presented in this section—there are plenty of idea-provoking designs and interesting materials to work with.

Whether you decide on a simple project or one of the more ambitious constructions, the rugged design, easy-to-find materials, and ready adaptability are all there. All projects fall within the budget and capabilities of most woodworkers. And the simple techniques used to build these play centers will teach your children a lot about how things are put together.

So make one of these exciting units for your kids. You'll find variety enough to suit all interests and imaginations—and you'll make their outdoor space something really special.

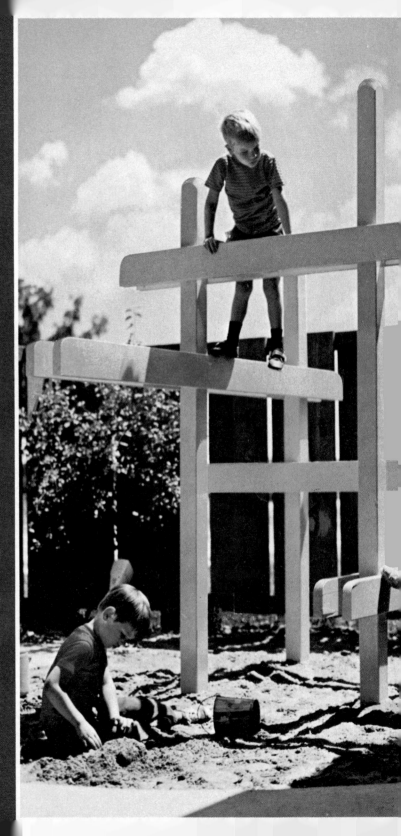

POST AND BEAM
FUN CENTER

Few backyard play units are easier to build than this one. And as your youngsters dream up endless ways to use it, you'll discover that few units are as versatile, either. To build it, bolt pairs of 2x8s to posts of varying heights. For finishing touches, paint the unit a bright color, hang a swing rope, and surround the base of the unit with clean sand.

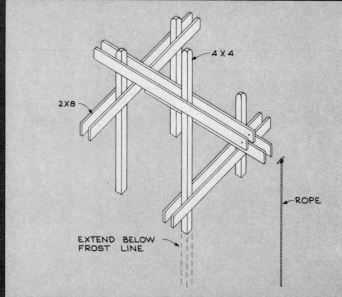

4 X 4

2X8

ROPE

EXTEND BELOW
FROST LINE

1 Treat bottoms of 4x4 posts with penta or creosote and allow to dry for two or three days. Dig postholes and anchor posts in concrete (see page 88). See sketch for placement of posts.
2 With saber saw, round off corners of 2x8 beams and sand smooth. Double-bolt two 2x8s to the tallest and shortest posts 15 inches from the ground. On opposite uprights, double-bolt two 2x8s four feet from the ground. (Check level of each 2x8 before drilling holes and bolting.)
3 At right angle to first two pairs of beams and at a height midway between them, double-bolt two 2x8s to tallest and shortest posts. On opposite uprights bolt two 2x8s about 6½ feet from the ground. Make sure to position the highest

pair of 2x8s so there will be plenty of clearance for the swing rope.
4 Paint or stain the unit.
5 At end of highest pair of 2x8s, drill a hole to accommodate a ½-inch bolt. Position a length of conduit between holes, with a washer between each end of the conduit and both 2x8s. Slide bolt through 2x8s, washers, and conduit. Secure bolt and attach a length of ¾-inch rope.

Materials (for project shown):
4x4 redwood—44 ft.
| 1 13 ft. 6 in. | 1 10 ft. |
| 1 11 ft. 6 in. | 1 96 in. |

2x8 redwood—74 ft.
| 2 96 in. | 2 9 ft. 6 in. |
| 2 9 ft. | 2 10 ft. |

Penta, paint or stain, length of conduit, and some ¾ inch rope.

TWO-STORY PLAY UNIT

This portable unit offers double-decked play areas for young backyard climbers. Build it easily with simple 2x4 and plywood framing. A piece of sturdy canvas stretched tightly over two hose-wrapped, spring-mounted chains provides a pretend hill that also shades the sandbox below. Paint the unit with bright enamel for protection from the elements.

1 Cut plywood pieces according to materials list. Cut an arc from one of the 30-inch-wide plywood pieces, and circular handholds from two others (see sketch).

2 From redwood, cut four 2x4 uprights, one end piece, and two 2x2s for top railings.

3 Paint the wood or treat it with weathering oil.

4 Screw top two plywood panels to rear pair of 2x4 uprights. Attach arc-shaped piece to front pair of uprights at the same level as the lower rear crosspiece (see sketch).

5 Join the two pairs of uprights by attaching the 2x2 top rails and the plywood panels with handholds to the uprights.

6 Nail the plywood base to the uprights as shown.

7 Attach remaining panels to unit, and nail the 2x4 at the front of the slide into position between plywood panels.

8 Wrap the two chains with lengths of split garden hose. Attach the springs to the chain and fasten to the unit with eyebolts.

9 Secure canvas to bottom chain, pull tightly over top chain, and secure to plywood.

Materials (for project shown):
¾-in. ext. plywood—1½ shts.
  2 84x9 in.   1 30x4 in.
  6 30x9 in.   1 30x30 in.
2x4 redwood—28 ft.
  4 70 in.   1 30 in.
2x2 redwood—6 ft.
  2 30 in.
Four eyebolts, two chains, 26 in.x10 ft. piece of canvas, discarded garden hose, two springs, and weathering oil or paint.

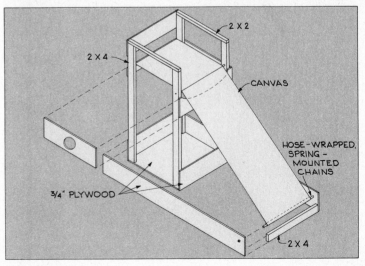

2 X 2

2 X 4

CANVAS

HOSE-WRAPPED, SPRING-MOUNTED CHAINS

¾" PLYWOOD

2 X 4

MULTI-LEVEL PLAYHOUSE

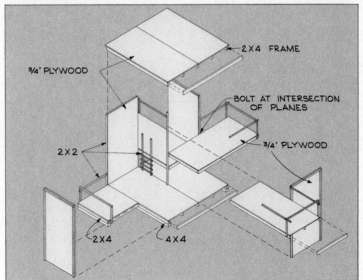

A simple cube built from plywood and two-inch framing will provide the scene for hours of sheltered play. Four cantilevered decks linked by ladders and steps—along with the various entries—result in a versatile, sure-to-be-used play area.

1 Stain or paint all surfaces, or treat with weathering oil. Set blocks in an 8-foot square. Check level and add 4x4 posts to adjust height if necessary.

2 For floor, build frame with two 96-inch 2x4s joined to two 93-inch 2x4s. Nail three 93-inch 2x4s on edge inside frame, with one in center to support joint of plywood pieces. Glue and nail two 4x8-foot plywood sheets to floor. Make side deck similarly with ½ sheet of plywood. Toenail to side of floor.

3 To build decks, nail two 96-inch 2x4s to two 45-inch 2x4s, then center and nail one 93-inch 2x4 on edge inside frame. Glue and nail a 4x8-foot sheet of plywood to frame. Make two more decks.

4 Glue and nail 2x2s to top and sides of four 4x8-foot sheets of plywood for walls. Beginning with lowest deck, check level and double-bolt decks to 2x2s on wall panels and center 2x2 upright as indicated in drawing.

5 Build roof the same as floor and nail in place.

6 Nail 2x2s to each deck for railing. Build ladder of two 48-inch 2x2 uprights and four 18-inch 2x2 rungs. Nail the ladder to the deck and toenail to the floor.

Materials (for project shown):
¾-in. ext. plywood—11½ shts.

3/4" PLYWOOD

2X4 FRAME

BOLT AT INTERSECTION OF PLANES

3/4" PLYWOOD

2 X 2

2 X 4

4 X 4

2x2 redwood—182 ft.

6	48 in.	8	24 in.
9	94½ in.	2	48 in.
11	51 in.	4	18 in.

2x4 redwood—228 ft.

10	96 in.	2	48 in.
13	93 in.	3	46½ in.
6	45 in.		

4x4 redwood—20 ft.

2	96 in.	1	48 in.

Exterior glue and paint, stain, or weathering oil, concrete blocks.

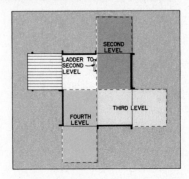

LADDER TO SECOND LEVEL

SECOND LEVEL

THIRD LEVEL

FOURTH LEVEL

DO-IT-ALL
JUNGLE
GYM

If your children love climbing, swinging, and jumping (don't they all!), you'll find it hard to tear them away from this roomy play structure. It's a challenge to build, but your efforts will yield high dividends in the many hours your kids will enjoy. For a finishing touch, fly a bright flag from the highest pole.

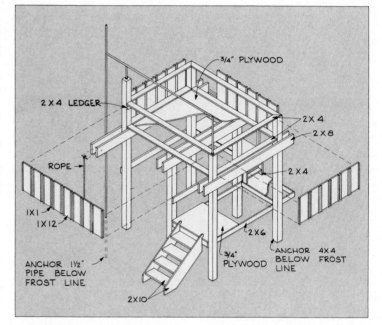

1 Treat bottoms of posts with penta and allow to dry for two or three days. Following sketch for positioning, dig postholes and set posts in concrete as directed on page 88. Make sure the three shorter corner posts are the same height. (For greater stability, brace with crossed 2x4s bolted to uprights.)

2 Double-bolt the 2x8s to uprights as shown, checking position with level before securing. Cut and fit sheets of ¾-inch plywood for top deck; secure with nails. (For greater stability, use tongue-and-groove flooring instead of plywood for top deck.)

3 Nail 2x4 ledger blocks to highest post to match height of other corner posts. Miter 2x4s and nail to tops of uprights and to ledger blocks on corner post.

4 For wall around deck, nail pieces of 1x12 to railings, and pieces of 1x1 to 1x12s.

5 To build lower decks, bolt 8-foot 6-inch 2x6s to uprights, extending length to rear. Toenail, bolt, or nail 2x6 floor supports to 2x6s or uprights as shown. Cut plywood pieces to fit and nail to 2x6s.

6 On center deck, bolt vertical 2x2 rail supports to 2x6 and bolt 2x4 railing to vertical supports.

7 Assemble ladder with 2x4 uprights and rungs, nail to 2x6s, and toenail to lower deck.

8 For front stairs, notch the 2x10s and cut at an angle at opposite ends so that they rest flat on the ground. Nail 2x10 stair treads to 2x10s at equal intervals, and nail stair unit to lowest deck.

9 Paint or stain unit.

10 On ground, assemble pipes in position shown in sketch. Dig posthole for vertical pipe, attach assembly to uprights with pipe fittings, and anchor pipe in concrete for stability. Drill holes in longest pair of 2x8s, attach ½-inch bolt covered with conduit, and hang swing rope.

Materials (for project shown):
4x4 posts—82 ft.
  1 16 ft.   2 11 ft. 6 in.
  3 14 ft.
¾-in. exterior plywood 6 shts.
2x10 redwood—22 ft.
  4 24 in.   2 78 in.
2x8 redwood—64 ft.
  4 9 ft.   2 11 ft.
2x6 redwood—54 ft.
  4 8 ft.   2 60 in.
  3 39 in.

2x4 redwood—82 ft.
  4 10 ft.
  4 84 in.
  2 24 in.
  3 16 in.
  1 60 in.
  2 3½ in.
2x2 redwood—6 ft.
  2 36 in.
1x12 redwood—66 ft.
  28 28 in.
1x1 redwood—132 ft.
  56 28 in.
1½-in. galvanized pipe—32 ft.
  1 36 in.   3 96 in.
  1 12 in.   2 24 in.
Two 1½-inch pipe tees, one 1½-inch elbow, two 1½-inch collars, penta or creosote, length of ¾-inch rope, conduit, and exterior paint or stain.

BACKYARD WATCHTOWER

Be prepared for visits from all the neighborhood kids when you decide to build this rugged play unit. And don't be surprised if they make the area beneath the platform their clubhouse.

1 Treat post bottoms with penta. Dig holes and set posts in concrete as directed on page 88.
2 For walls, nail a 2x4 between top of second highest post and ledger nailed to highest post. Nail a 2x4 to tops of third highest posts and to ledger nailed to corner post. Toenail 2x4s between posts on longest wall. Nail plywood to wall.
3 On other wall, nail ledger blocks at bottom and nail 2x4 to ledgers. Nail plywood to this wall.
4 Bolt 2x6 ledgers to posts, and bolt 2x6s to posts for ladder.
5 For handrail, nail a 1x4 to shortest post; toenail to ladder post.
6 Nail fence posts to 2x6s.
7 Paint or stain unit.

Materials: (for project shown):
4x4 redwood or cedar—56 ft.

2 12 ft.	2 90 in.
1 8 ft. 6 in.	1 72 in.

2x6 redwood—56 ft.

7 42 in.	3 48 in.
1 11 ft.	1 41 in.

2x4 redwood—24 ft.

1 41 in.	1 92½ in.
3 3 in.	1 25½ in.
1 6 in.	1 44½ in.
1 60 in.	

½-in. ext. plywood—1½ shts.

1 48x58 in.	1 24x96 in.

1x4 redwood—6 ft.

1 63½ in.

Half-round fence posts—144 ft.

12 40 in.	12 92 in.

Paint or stain, and penta.

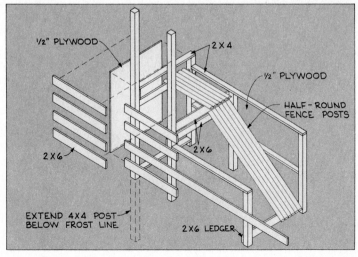

½" PLYWOOD
2 X 4
½" PLYWOOD
HALF-ROUND FENCE POSTS
2 X 6
2 X 6
EXTEND 4X4 POST BELOW FROST LINE
2 X 6 LEDGER

A-FRAME
PLAY SHELTER

This angular unit is a breeze to build, using standard-size materials and simple construction methods. The shelter looks the same when viewed from either side and will offer limitless play possibilities for children of all ages. Just set two posts, nail sides together, and add roof—then let the kids take over.

1 Treat 4x4 posts with penta and allow to dry for two or three days. Dig postholes 6 feet apart and set posts in concrete as directed on page 88. For best results, it's best to select a spot where the ground is absolutely level. Stain all of the remaining wood.

2 For the side sections, align the long 1x8s side by side. Nail a 1x4 to both ends of the 1x8s. Measuring from the same edge, mark off 5 feet along the top edge and 10 feet along the bottom edge. Draw a line between these two marks. Nail a 1x4 into each of the 1x8s on both sides of the line. Then, cut the 1x8s into two pieces along this line, between the 1x4s.

3 To assemble roof sections, align two groups of 1x8s, and nail a 1x4 to each end.

4 To assemble the unit, nail side sections to the posts so that the 7-foot sides of the sections are resting on the ground. Make absolutely sure that each side piece is nailed to the upright at the same angle. If you fail to do this, the roof sections will not lie correctly when the unit is assembled.

5 Position each roof section on both sides of unit and nail to side sections.

Materials (for project shown):
4x4 redwood—20 ft.
    2 8 ft. 6 in.
1x4 redwood—46 ft.
    6 58 in.
    2 82 in.
1x8 redwood—224 ft.
    16 72 in.
    8 15 ft.
Penta preservative or creosote, and exterior stain.

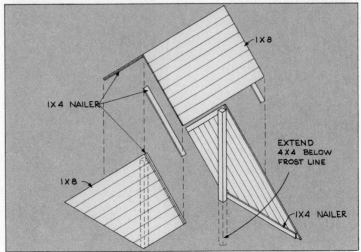

1X4 NAILER

1X8

1X8

EXTEND
4X4 BELOW
FROST LINE

1X4 NAILER

EASY OUTDOOR STORAGE

Convenience . . . that's the big plus outdoor storage units have to offer. They provide safe, year-round niches for lawn furniture, barbecue equipment, yard tools, and even bicycles—right where they're needed and used. Best of all, you save valuable indoor storage space at the same time.

Try one or more of the easy-to-build projects in this chapter. Each storage unit is designed for function and beauty—and they're plenty rugged to stand up to all kinds of weather.

Start by deciding which of the designs will best serve your needs. Then modify any of them to suit your special requirements.

Use the materials list that accompanies each project as a guide to how much lumber you'll need to finish the job. You probably have some of the necessary materials already on hand. Purchase other items from your local building supply store.

With the step-by-step instructions, the rest is easy. All you have to do is choose a location for your project and put your carpentry skills to work!

FIREWOOD STORAGE BIN

Keep your firewood neat and dry inside this upright storage bin. You can build it in just a few hours by constructing a frame of redwood 2x4s and nailing on ⅝-inch exterior plywood siding. The lower storage compartment is an especially handy place to stash charcoal, small lawn equipment, or garden supplies.

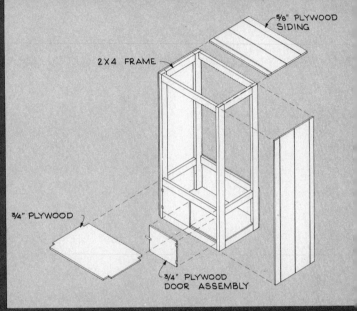

5/8" PLYWOOD SIDING

2 X 4 FRAME

3/4" PLYWOOD

3/4" PLYWOOD DOOR ASSEMBLY

1 Construct the redwood frame by gluing and nailing 2x4s together with simple butt joints (see sketch). Treat the bottom row of 2x4s with penta; allow to dry.
2 Cut two pieces of ¾-inch exterior plywood to form the bottom of each storage area. Cut out the corners of the plywood pieces to fit around the 2x4 frame, then nail in place as shown.
3 Nail sections of ⅝-inch exterior plywood siding to the frame. First, nail the top panel into place; then attach the side panels, making sure they are flush with the top of the unit. Allow a ⅝-inch space between the ground and the bottom of each side panel.
4 Nail the back of the lower storage area into place, again allowing a small space at the bottom.
5 Stain or paint the unit.
6 Cut two identical ¾-inch plywood panels to serve as doors. Paint or stain the pieces; then flush-mount each door with galvanized butt hinges. Add a hasp lock to secure the doors.

Materials (for a 3x2x6-foot bin)
⅝-in. plywood siding—1½ shts.
  2 24x72 in.   1 24x36 in.
  1 36x18⅜ in.
¾-in. exterior plywood—½ sht.
  1 23¼x36 in.   1 24x36 in.
  2 12x16½ in.
2x4 redwood—52 ft.
  4 72 in.   6 17 in.
  6 33 in.
Glue, four butt hinges, hasp lock, penta, and stain or paint.

STORAGE/ SERVING CENTER

This brightly painted snack bar/storage unit Is also a great piece of patio furniture. Ceramic tiles make up the easy-to-clean countertop, and the roomy storage area below provides a dry home for stackable outdoor furniture. Above, the wall-mounted storage shelf keeps glassware and dishes close at hand for carefree outdoor entertaining.

1 Start by building the large storage base unit. With simple butt joints, build 2x2 frames for the front, sides, and top of the unit.

2 Cut ¾-inch plywood panels to fit the 2x2 frame for the top, sides, and doors of the storage bar. Nail the side panels into the frame as indicated; then, nail on the plywood top. (Wait until later to hang the cabinet doors and lay the ceramic tiles.)

3 To build the 6-foot back wall, toenail together three sides of the 2x4 frame with butt joints. (Cross-brace the frame with scrap lumber during construction.)

4 Glue and nail quarter round trim strips into position to serve as stops, mitering corners.

5 Precut 1x2s, 1x6s, and 1x8s to form the back wall, mitering both ends of each board at a 45 degree angle. In sequence, slide a 1x8 followed by a 1x6 and a 1x2 into the frame, butting one against the other. Repeat the procedure until the back wall is complete. (If desired, use tongue-and-groove lumber to build the back wall.)

6 As soon as the back wall is in position, nail on the fourth side of the 2x4 frame and the final strips of quarter round.

7 Attach the previously assembled storage bar to the back wall by fitting it into position and nailing into place.

8 Build the long "box" for the upper storage area from 1x10s butted together. Attach the box to the back wall at a convenient height. Precut sliding doors from ¼-inch hardboard.

9 Paint or stain project and allow to dry. Separately, paint or stain

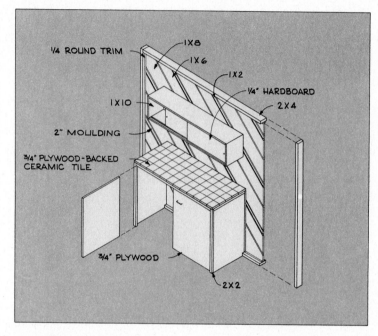

doors for both upper and lower storage areas and allow to dry.

10 Hang the lower unit's doors using two butt hinges for each. Add magnetic catches so the doors close flush.

11 Affix sliding door guides on the upper storage unit. Slip hardboard doors into place.

12 To lay the ceramic tile countertop, prime plywood with sealer. Apply adhesive with notched spreader. Press tiles into place. After a day or two, grout joints.

Materials (for a 30x48x46-inch lower cabinet, a 9¼x48x12-inch upper cabinet, and a 6-foot back wall):

¾-inch ext. plywood—1½ shts.
  1 30x48 in.   2 27x33½ in.
  2 22½x33 in.

¼-inch hardboard
  2 10¼x24 in.

1x2 pine or redwood—40 ft.

1x6 pine or redwood—40 ft.

1x8 pine or redwood—40 ft.

1x10 pine or redwood—10 ft.
  2 46½ in.   2 12 in.

2x4 pine or redwood—24 ft.
  4 72 in.

2x2 pine or redwood—24 ft.
  2 45 in.   2 35¼ in.
  2 33¾ in.   2 27 in.

Quarter round—44 ft.
  7 72 in.   2 12 in.

Two 48-inch sliding door guides; 77 4½x4½-inch ceramic tiles; exterior glue; tile primer, adhesive, and grout; four butt hinges; two magnetic catches; two cabinet door handles; and paint or stain.

BACKYARD STORAGE CENTER

This striking storage module/ serving bar is roomy enough for all of your outdoor furniture, barbecue equipment, and entertaining supplies. The large six-foot-wide door swings open on a smooth-rolling caster to double as a privacy screen. And you'll find the fold-down countertop invaluable at backyard barbecues, as a serving center, or as an extra work surface.

1 Start construction by building the 2x4 frame. Cut redwood 2x4s to size, measuring angles and mitering corners to fit the angular design shown in the sketches. Pretreat with penta any 2x4s that will sit on the ground.

2 Toenail the 2x4 frame together with butt joints. For strength, use scrap lumber as cross braces during construction. Wait until later to build the frame for the caster-mounted door.

3 Line inside of cabinet section with ½-inch plywood panels cut to size. Line the sides first; then, add plywood panels to top and bottom and nail in place.

4 Install ½-inch plywood shelves; use lengths of 2x2s as ledgers. Wait to install the fold-down countertop and the cabinet doors.

5 Precut enough ⅝-inch plywood siding to cover the entire 2x4 frame of the storage center.

6 One-by-one (starting with the sides), nail siding panels into place. Panel the 2x4 frame both outside and inside. Nail the large top into place last.

7 Mount 2x2s on angle braces; affix to inside wall as shown. Nail 1x1 door stop into position.

8 Paint or stain the storage center.

9 To build the large door, toenail together the 2x4 frame using butt joints. Cut ⅝-inch plywood siding panels to fit the door frame and nail them into position.

10 Install a ball-type caster under one corner of the door.

11 Paint or stain the door and let dry. Then, attach door assembly to storage unit frame with three large door hinges.

12 To install the fold-down door,

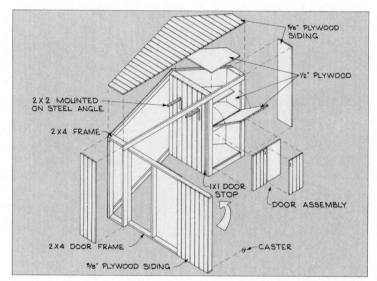

cut ½-inch plywood to size and face it with ⅝-inch siding. Paint or stain the door and hang it with two butt hinges. Secure door with two lengths of chain.

13 Construct the lower cabinet doors from plywood faced with siding. Paint or stain the doors before installing. Then, screw them into place using T-hinges.

14 Install handles on all doors.

Materials (for project shown):
⅝-inch plywood siding—12 shts.
½-inch plywood—4 shts.
2x4 redwood—184 ft.

1	9 ft.	1	84 in.
2	48 in.	1	77 in.
2	25½ in.	6	57 in.
12	53½ in.	4	48 in.
2	30 in.	4	54 in.
2	72 in.		

2x2 redwood—14 ft.

3	12 in.	2	24 in.

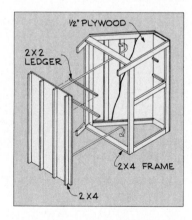

1	6 in.	2	36 in.

1x1 redwood doorstop—4 ft.
  1 48 in.
Glue, chain, four T-hinges, two butt hinges, three door hinges, two steel angle braces, one ball-type caster, door handles, and paint or stain.

FLIP-TOP STORAGE BENCH

It's easy to build this sturdy bench from rustic redwood and ¾-inch plywood panels. Here, twin hinged tops fold back for easy access to two large storage areas . . . perfect spots to keep children's bats, baseballs, and other recreation paraphernalia. If desired, decorate the bench with colorful throw cushions to make it even more attractive and comfortable.

1 Construct bench frame from 4x4 uprights and 2x2 rails. Toenail each 2x2 rail flush against the inside edges of the 4x4 posts.

2 Face the inside surfaces of the redwood frame with ½-inch exterior plywood panels. Leave a ½-inch gap in the middle for a divider.

3 Use a single piece of plywood for the bottom and nail into place. Butt 1x1 reinforcing strips against frame and underside of bottom panel for strength.

4 Slide the plywood divider into the box, nailing it into place.

5 Glue and nail evenly spaced 2x2 verticals all around the bench.

6 Stain bench, or treat with oil.

7 Construct the top panels. Before assembling, groove the long 2x2 slats with small notches for drainage (see sketch). Alternate long slats with 2x2 spacers, gluing and nailing together as you go.

8 Back the redwood top panels with ½-inch plywood. Stain or treat with weathering oil. When dry, hinge each top panel to the outside edge of the 4x4 uprights.

Materials (for a 72x25½x18-inch bench):

½-in. ext. plywood—1½ shts.
- 3 12¾x17½ in.   4 12¾x33 in.
- 1 18½x66½ in.   2 35x24½ in.

4x4 redwood—10 ft.
- 6 16½ in.

2x2 redwood—152 ft.
- 8 30¾ in.   16 33 in.
- 4 18½ in.   4 22½ in.
- 38 11 in.   28 6 in.
- 4 36 in.

1x1 redwood—16 ft.
- 2 66½ in.   2 17 in.

Exterior glue, four butt hinges, and stain or weathering oil.

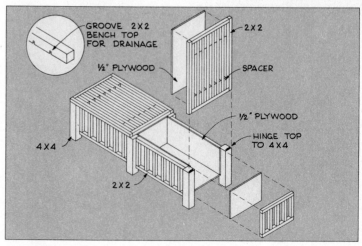

GROOVE 2X2 BENCH TOP FOR DRAINAGE

2 X 2

½" PLYWOOD

SPACER

½" PLYWOOD

HINGE TOP TO 4 X 4

4 X 4

2 X 2

BARBECUE HIDE-ALL

Wouldn't it be great to keep your barbecue equipment out of sight (and out of the weather!) when it's not in use? Here's the ideal project to do it—a storage cabinet that not only hides your grill, but also all of your charcoal, cooking utensils, lighter fluid, and other outdoor cooking necessities. Build it in an afternoon and use it that evening . . . it's that easy to construct!

1 Cut out the sides, top, back, shelves, and doors from plywood.
2 Glue and nail 1x4 base supports to the left side and back panels (see sketch). Construct a cabinet base by butting 1x2s together; nail bottom shelf of cabinet/drawer assembly onto 1x2 frame.
3 Nail the side, back, and top panels into position. Nail the bottom shelf assembly onto the side and back panels (see sketch).
4 Attach the front plywood face to complete the shell of the cabinet/drawer section.
5 Nail 1x1 shelf ledgers into place and install shelves.
6 Paint or stain unit before hanging doors and building drawer.
7 Cut out pieces of ¾-inch plywood for the drawer. Butt-join and attach drawer guides.
8 Paint or stain drawer and the cabinet doors; let dry. Hang front and side doors using two butt hinges per door. Attach a catch and handle to each door.

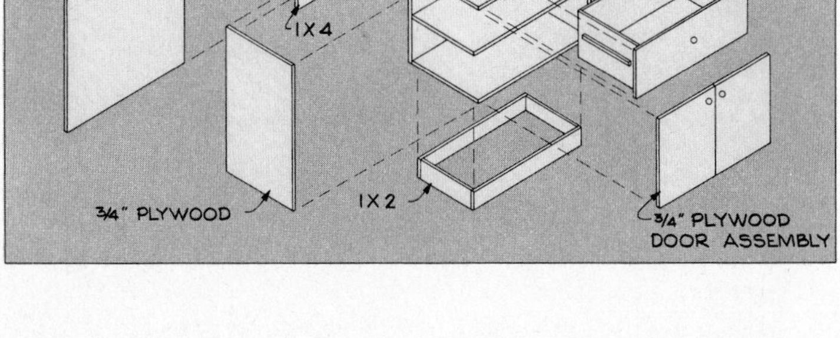

Materials (48x30x36-inch cabinet):

¾-in. exterior plywood—3 shts.
1 48x30 in.	3 29¼x33¾ in.
1 48x33¾ in.	2 28½x17¼ in.
1 28½x16½ in.	1 18x33¾ in.
2 21¼x14¼ in.	1 28½x11 in.
2 15x11 in.	1 25½x11 in.
1 25½x13½ in.	

1x4 redwood—6 ft.
  2 28½ in.

1x2 redwood—8 ft.
  2 14 in.   2 28 in.

1x1 redwood ledgers—6 ft.
  2 16½ in.   2 17¼ in.

Exterior glue, six butt hinges, drawer guides, magnetic catches, door handles, and paint or stain.

Labels in diagram: ¾" PLYWOOD, ¾" PLYWOOD, DRAWER GUIDE, DRAWER ASSEMBLY, 1X4, ¾" PLYWOOD, 1X2, ¾" PLYWOOD DOOR ASSEMBLY

PROJECTS FOR BACKYARD GET-TOGETHERS

Fun is the name of the game come summertime, and one of the best places to enjoy the season is your own backyard.

You'll find that all of these projects are designed with outdoor fun in mind. From the sleek, quick-to-build deck table to the colorful roll-around serving cart, each will dress up your backyard, deck, or patio in style.

You can build some of these items and begin enjoying them all in the same afternoon. Others, such as the U-shaped serving center and the magnificent gazebo, will take a little time.

It's easy to get started. Just pick out your favorite projects and analyze your yard space and needs to determine if any construction details need altering. Then gather your materials and start in. You'll find that with the step-by-step instructions and handy project pointers, all you'll need to turn out professional results are a few simple tools and some patience.

EASY-REACH BARBECUE TABLE

Gather the group around this intriguing table and have a cook-your-own barbecue party. Here, brightly painted tractor seats (they're comfortable!) are perched atop 6x6 posts. Thick, rugged bridge planks run underfoot, with splashes of flowers and greenery to make the scene as cheerful as a sunny summer day.

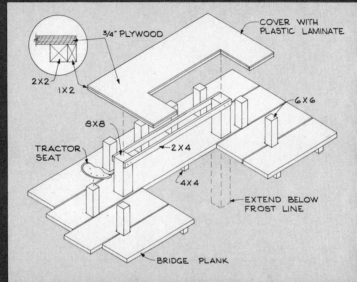

1 Pretreat seat and table supports with penta and allow to dry. Dig postholes, insert posts, and anchor in concrete (see page 88).
2 Nail two 2x4 rails to the 8x8 support posts as shown. Cut out the tabletop from plywood.
3 Before mounting, glue and nail 2x2 reinforcing strips around the underside of the top, ¾ inch from the edge. Then, face the 2x2s with 1x2s (see sketch).
4 Nail top to 8x8 posts and to 2x4 rails. Cover top and sides with plastic laminate.
5 Stain all exposed wood areas, or treat with weathering oil.
6 Pretreat 4x4s with penta.
7 Cut bridge planks to fit around the seat and table supports.
8 Nail planks to 4x4 stabilizers.
9 Paint the tractor seats; nail or screw onto 6x6 posts.

Materials (for an 8-foot table):
Miscellaneous bridge planks
¾-in. exterior plywood—1 sht.
8x8 redwood—10 ft.
  2 60 in.
6x6 redwood—48 ft.
  8 54 in.
4x4 redwood—enough to secure planks
2x4 redwood—16 ft.
  2 84 in.
2x2 redwood—30 ft.
  2 14½ in.   2 46½ in.
  2 22¾ in.
  1 59½ in.
  1 91½ in.
1x2 redwood—30 ft.
  1 96 in.   2 46½ in.
  1 58 in.   2 22 in.
  2 19 in.
Plastic laminate and adhesive, penta, glue, eight tractor seats, stain or weathering oil, and paint

LOW-PROFILE DECK TABLE

Add some style to your deck or patio with this sleek table arrangement. The design shown here is only a foot high (18 inches at the center supports), but you can easily adapt it to any height that suits you. Then scatter a few colorful cushions, and enjoy some table-side relaxation. Now *that's* living.

1 Determine how tall you want your deck table to be. Then, cut the two vertical center supports for the table from a redwood 2x10. Cut another section of 2x10 to lay flat between the center supports and nail in place (see sketch).

2 Nail two identical lengths of redwood 2x4 to the center supports at the desired height. (Cut the 2x4s long enough so they will extend beyond the width of the tabletop as shown).

3 Treat the table frame assembly with weathering oil, stain, or paint. Separately, cut out three lengths of a redwood 2x10 to serve as the large, flat table surface. Stain, paint, or treat them with weathering oil to match the table frame.

4 Glue and nail the tabletop pieces to the frame. Inset the nail heads and cover the holes with a wood filler.

Materials (for project shown):
2x10 redwood—12 ft.
  3 30 in.
  1 9½ in.
  2 18 in.
2x4 redwood—6 ft.
  2 36 in.
Exterior glue, wood filler, and paint, stain, or weathering oil.

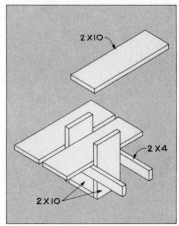

U-SHAPED SERVING CENTER

Is lack of outdoor counter space cramping your barbecue style? If so, this roomy serving center/storage unit is the answer. The design shown has built-in drawers to supplement the large countertop work area. And for even more space, you can install doors beneath the countertop. Either way, you'll want to station your grill within easy reach of this handy project.

1 Construct a frame from 2x4s toenailed together and cross-braced with scrap lumber during construction. (To make this unit freestanding, add 8 inches in height to all vertical 2x4s and siding. Let unit rest on its frame.)
2 Attach drawer guides to frame.
3 Nail siding to the front, sides, and back of the frame. Then, nail on the top panels, framing all around the top with 1x4s. NOTE: You can modify construction to include cabinets. Line the interior of the frame with ½-inch plywood and hang doors made from siding.
4 Construct drawers by butting the sides to a plywood bottom and facing each drawer with ½-inch siding. Add drawer glides.
5 Paint or stain the entire unit. Screw on drawer handles.

Materials (for unit shown):
½-inch plywood siding—3 shts.
  1 25½x48 in.   2 37½x18 in.
  2 36x28 in.   2 28x48 in.
  4 18x28 in.   6 6x14 in.
  2 3x14 in.
½-in. plywood—½ sht.
  8 10½x16¼ in.
2x4 redwood—76 ft.
  12 21 in.   6 15 in.
  8 36 in.   1 91 in.
  3 48 in.
1x6 redwood—26 ft.
  12 17 in.   6 10½ in.
1x4 redwood—26 ft.
  1 91 in.   1 48 in.
  4 19½ in.   2 36 in.
1x3 redwood—8 ft.
  4 17 in.   2 10½ in.
Galvanized drawer guides
  16 17½ in.   16 17 in.
Exterior glue, drawer handles, and paint or stain.

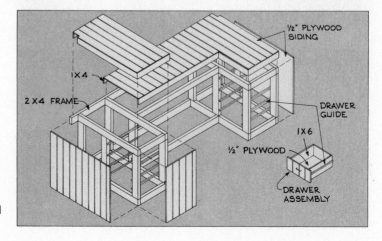

½" PLYWOOD SIDING
1X4
2 X 4 FRAME
DRAWER GUIDE
1X6
½" PLYWOOD
DRAWER ASSEMBLY

GUEST-PLEASING GAZEBO

This eye-catching unit is so well constructed and professional looking, your friends won't believe you built it yourself. It's a natural for airy, summer relaxing and the perfect focal point in heavily vegetated landscapes. Here, evergreens and other foliage surround the structure, and geraniums in a textured planter add a splash of color.

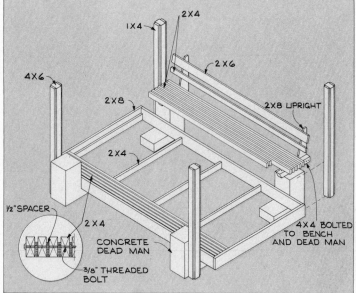

1 Build this structure from the ground up. NOTE: Apply stain or weathering oil to all wood surfaces *before* assembly.

2 First, make a wooden form to cast the concrete piers (dead men). Use steel reinforcing rods to strengthen the concrete. Also set two threaded reinforcing rods extending from the top and another extending from the outside face of each dead man (you'll use them to bolt on the bench and roof supports).

3 After the dead men are cast and hardened, position them the proper distance apart on a level area. They do not have to be buried in the ground.

4 Start building the deck floor by making the outer frame from 2x8s. Nail together with butt joints.

5 Nail 2x4 ledgers to the frame, flush with the bottom edge of the 2x8s as shown in the sketch.

6 Cut all of your 2x4 decking boards to size. Also cut 3x3-inch spacer strips from a sheet of ½-inch plywood. Drill three holes in each 2x4 and each spacer in identical locations, large enough for a ⅜-inch threaded bolt (see sketch detail).

7 Nail the floor of the deck into place, taking care to line up the three predrilled holes as you go. Then, drill holes in two sides of the 2x8 frame to line up with the holes in the decking. Insert a long, threaded ⅜-inch bolt into each hole and bolt the deck planks to the 2x8 frame.

8 Build the benches onto the concrete dead men. Start by bolting

(continued)

GUEST-PLEASING GAZEBO

(continued)

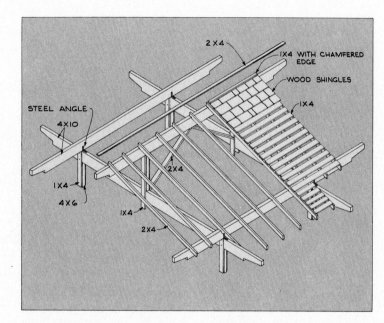

for shingles (see sketch). If desired, cover 1x4s with roofing felt before laying the roof.

16 Shingle the roof.

17 Finish the apex of the roof with two chamfered 1x4s extending the length of the roof and topped by a 2x4 extending beyond the edge of the roof on both sides.

Materials (for the deck and benches):

½-in. exterior plywood—½ sheet
  153 3x3 in.

2x8 redwood—44 ft.
  2 72 in.   2 11 ft.
  4 24 in.

4x4 redwood—8 ft.
  4 24 in.

2x6 redwood—20 ft.
  2 9 ft.

2x4 redwood—646 ft.
  16 9 ft.   38 11 ft.
  5 69 in.

(for roof and roof supports):

4x10 redwood—84 ft.
  2 17 ft.   3 15 ft.

4x6 redwood—40 ft.
  4 9 ft.

4x4 redwood—6 ft.
  2 36 in.

2x4 redwood—250 ft.
  8 9 ft.   12 11 ft.
  2 60 in.   1 15 ft.

1x4 redwood—618 ft.
  8 10 ft.   4 54 in.
  10 72 in.   38 12 ft.

Concrete for four dead men with steel reinforcing rods, 1½ squares of wood shingles, exterior glue, three 74-inch-long ⅜-inch diameter threaded bolts, six 11½-inch-long ⅜-inch diameter threaded bolts, steel angle braces, miscellaneous bolts, roofing felt, and stain or weathering oil.

a 4x4 onto the preset threaded reinforcing rods on top of each dead man. Then, cut out the 2x8 angled back supports for each bench as shown. Bolt the 2x8 supports to the 4x4s.

9 Nail a 2x6 and a 2x4 crosspiece to each 2x8 back support to form the back of the bench.

10 To make the bench seats, drill holes in 2x4s and ½-inch spacers as you did for the deck floor. Bolt the bench seats together with ⅜-inch bolts inserted through the holes. Then, attach each seat assembly to the 4x4 bench supports with steel angle braces.

11 Install the tall roof supports by bolting a 4x6 to each dead man as shown—again, bolting to a preset threaded reinforcing rod.

12 Glue and nail 1x4s to two faces of each 4x6 column, extending each 1x4 beyond the end of the 4x6 as shown in sketch. Then, attach the long 4x10 roof support beams between the exposed tops of the 1x4s. Use heavy bolts to secure the 1x4s to the beams.

13 Before installing remaining three 4x10 roof beams, precut dadoes in each beam to hold 2x4 rafters. Then, attach outer two beams to 4x10s beneath them with steel angle braces as shown. To install center top beam, build two vertical center supports from 4x4s faced with 1x4s as shown. Toenail center beam to 4x4 supports, and then cross-brace beam with mitered 2x4s (see sketch).

14 One by one, toenail the 2x4 rafters into place.

15 Nail long 1x4 slats into place

PATIO CHUCK WAGON

Let the good times roll with this entertainment center on wheels. Constructed mainly of ¾-inch plywood, the cart features a cutting board work surface fashioned from tongue-and-groove oak flooring. Storage areas above and below hold plenty of glasses, dishes, and refreshments. And the large rear wheels make the going easy over your backyard terrain.

1 Construct the body of the cart from pieces of plywood. Cut two large pieces to serve as the bottoms for the upper and lower storage compartments. Nail two center dividers into place. Follow with plywood end pieces for the top storage bays.

2 Cut out the large side panels for the cart in the shape shown.

3 Nail one of the side panels into place. Then, install sliding door guides at both ends of the frame.

4 Cut doors to size. Paint entire unit.

5 When dry, install the sliding doors into the guides and nail on the second side of the cart.

6 Install 1x2 crosspieces for the front wheel assembly. Then, install the pull handle.

7 Nail 1x1 ledgers into position and follow with oak flooring to form top of cart. Seal and varnish the flooring; allow to dry.

8 Install the front casters and the large rear wheels as shown.

Materials (for project shown):
¾-inch ext. plywood—2 shts.
  2 36x52 in.   2 36x22½ in.
  1 16x22½ in.   3 6x22½ in.
1x1 redwood—6 ft.
  4 16½ in.
1x2 redwood—4 ft.
  2 22½ in.
¼-inch hardboard—½ sheet
  4 16x12 in.
1x3 tongue-and-groove oak flooring
1 in. wood dowel—3 ft.
  1 24 in.
Four 24-inch sliding door guides, glue, two casters, two wheels, axle and conduit, conduit brackets, paint, sealer, and varnish.

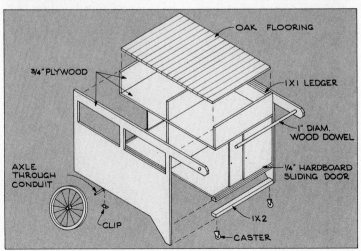

OAK FLOORING

¾" PLYWOOD

1X1 LEDGER

1" DIAM. WOOD DOWEL

¼" HARDBOARD SLIDING DOOR

AXLE THROUGH CONDUIT

CLIP

1X2

CASTER

COMPACT PATIO DECK

You'll love this economical deck for its simplicity and ease of installation. Build it from 2x4s laid flat within a 2x12 frame, and raise it slightly above ground level with 4x4s anchored in concrete. Then, landscape your deck/patio with low shrubs and multicolored flowers. You'll want to add comfortable lawn furniture for peaceful summertime relaxation.

1 Measure carefully for the correct location of all 4x4 posts. Dig postholes. Pretreat 4x4s with penta; then, set 4x4 posts into holes and anchor in concrete (see instructions for setting posts on page 88).
2 Build the deck frame by nailing 2x12s onto the 4x4 posts. Be sure the top edge of each 2x12 extends 1½ inches above the posts.
3 Attach 2x4 ledgers to the 2x12 frame as shown in the sketch. Then, nail parallel 2x6 joists onto the frame at even intervals.
4 Before nailing on the 2x4s for the deck top, spread redwood chips or gravel under and around the deck frame.
5 Paint, stain, or treat the frame with weathering oil.
6 Nail 2x4s into place to form the deck surface, butting one against the other or spacing each slightly apart from the next. Nail each 2x4 both to the joists and to the deck frame.
7 Paint, stain, or treat the 2x4 surface with weathering oil.
8 If desired, install a sliding glass door access to deck. Add potted flowers to help accent the natural look of the deck.

Materials (for a 10x10-foot deck):
4x4 redwood or fir—20 ft.
    4 54 in.
2x4 redwood or fir—280 ft.
    26 9 ft. 9 in.
     2 9 ft. 5 in.
2x12 redwood or fir—40 ft.
    4 10 ft.
2x6 redwood or fir—40 ft.
    4 10 ft.
Stain, exterior paint or weathering oil, and penta.

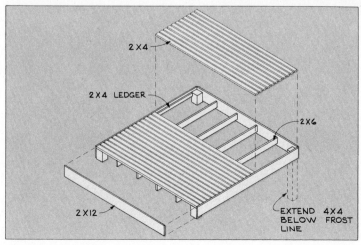

CONTEMPORARY PICNIC TABLE

Sitting down for a picnic-style summer meal is an American tradition. And here's a modern variation of the classic picnic table that's right at home in a corner of your deck or patio. It features a permanently placed L-shaped bench and a sleek matching table. You may want to construct extra freestanding bench sections to bring out for seating the whole gang.

1 Cut the frame for the tabletop. Miter corners at 45-degree angles and nail together. Nail on 2x4 ledgers, recessing each 1½-inches below top edge of frame.
2 Cut 2x6s to form the tabletop. Nail to ledgers.
3 Cut table legs from 2x4s and join them at the middle with lap joints. Miter both ends of each leg at a 45-degree angle. Then, cut two-piece center support from 2x4s, mitering each end as shown.
4 Nail all legs and supports into position. Strengthen each leg assembly at the lap joint by bolting it to the center support pieces. Nail on tabletop.
5 Paint or stain the table.
6 Construct bench frame of 1x6s and 2x4 ledgers (see sketch). Miter the corners of the 1x6 frame.
7 Cut 2x6s to form the L-shaped bench top. Nail to ledgers.
8 Using a steel plate welded to each end of a 3-inch pipe, bolt the bench legs to the bench and then to the patio or deck.
9 Paint or stain the bench.

Materials (for table and bench):
2x6 redwood—84 ft.
  3 12 ft. 6 in.   7 60 in.
1x6 redwood—50 ft.
  2 62 in.   2 42 in.
  1 90 in.   1 60 in.
  1 40 in.   1 80 in.
  2 20 in.
2x4 redwood—46 ft.
  4 52 in.   3 38½ in.
  5 16½ in.   1 28 in.
  2 39 in.
Six steel plates, three 16-inch sections of steel pipe (3-inch diameter, exterior glue, screws and bolts, and paint or stain.

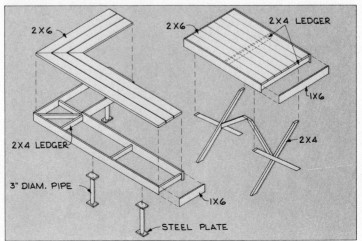

2X6   2X6   2X4 LEDGER

2X4 LEDGER

3" DIAM. PIPE

STEEL PLATE

1X6

1X6

2X4

PRIVACY SCREENS AND FENCES

It's just human nature to crave a place where you can relax and release yourself from the tensions of the outside world. So why not satisfy that urge by erecting one of the dramatic screens or fences presented here and on the following pages?

The projects in this chapter are easy to build yourself . . . and they are much less expensive to install than buying pre-built fence sections. You can construct most of them with a few simple tools and basic carpentry techniques, yet when finished they look entirely professional.

First, you'll want to choose a fence that blends well with the architectural lines of your home as well as with the style of your lawn or patio. Get started by planning the location of your fence. Then, determine how high and how long you want it to be. Also, check local ordinances about fence construction and discuss your plans with neighbors.

Now, let your imagination go! You can adapt any of the following project ideas to your own special needs and requirements.

REDWOOD AND CANVAS SCREEN

This economical privacy screen is fashioned from redwood 4x4s and colorful stretch canvas panels. Here, the frames are blocked with canvas replacement covers for garden reclining chairs, which come ready-made in kits, complete with lacing cord. This fence is 6 feet high and 12 feet long, but dimensions are adjustable.

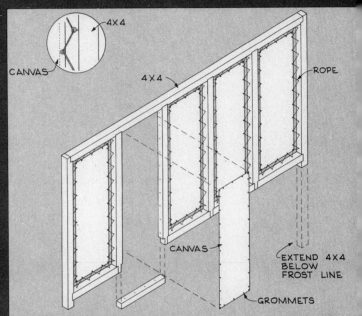

1 Determine location and length of fence. Figure 24½ inches for each canvas section (includes lacing) and 3½ inches for each 4x4.

2 Precut 4x4s to fit desired dimensions. Make 1-inch dado cuts (see page 92) and rabbet joints (see page 92) in advance as indicated in sketch. Treat posts with penta.

3 Dig postholes, measuring carefully for the correct location of each post. Insert posts and anchor in concrete (see page 88).

4 Fit the 4x4 top plate onto two support posts, gluing and nailing into the precut rabbet joints.

5 Complete the remainder of the frame section-by-section according to the sketch, gluing and nailing together as you go.

6 Screw eye hooks into the redwood frame (see sketch).

7 Stain, paint, or treat the frame with weathering oil.

8 Affix grommets at regular intervals along the borders of the panels (you'll need to rent or buy a hand-held grommet tool).

9 Lace panels to eye hooks on frame with rope (see sketch).

Materials (for a 12x6-foot fence)
4x4 redwood—68 ft.

| 4 | 70 in | 5 | 26½ in. |
| 2 | 10 ft. | 1 | 11 ft. 7 in. |

Five 18x60-inch pieces of light canvas, five 40-foot pieces of nylon rope, 130 grommets (metal eyelets), 130 hooks (eye screws), exterior glue, penta, and stain, paint, or weathering oil.

SNOW FENCE SCREEN

This airy privacy screen is economical yet rich in good looks. You can build it from prestained snow fencing nailed to a redwood frame. Check farm sales and auctions for sections of used snow fence . . . you may be able to pick up a bargain. Or, buy it new from your lumber supply outlet. For extra privacy, nail fencing to both sides of the 2x4 frame.

1 Pretreat the 4x4 support posts with penta and allow to dry. Dig postholes and set posts, anchoring in concrete (see instructions on page 88).

2 Attach 3½-inch ledgers cut from a redwood 2x4. Then, glue and nail 2x4 redwood crossmembers to the support posts as shown.

3 Stain frame before nailing up snow fence. Choose a color that closely matches the rustic red of the pre-stained slats.

4 Nail one row of fence to the lower portion of the frame, then a second above the first for sufficient height. (Take care to align the slats for the two rows as you install the upper section.)

5 If desired, nail fencing to other side of frame. Arrange slats on one side of fence opposite openings between slats on other side.

Materials (for an 8-foot section):
2x4 redwood—26 ft.
    3 92½ in.   6 3½ in.
4x4 redwood—24 ft.
    2 11 ft. 6 in.
Two 4x8-foot sections snow fence, exterior glue, penta, and stain.

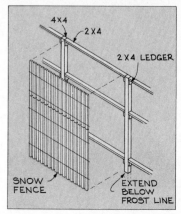

4x4

2 X 4

2 X 4 LEDGER

SNOW FENCE

EXTEND BELOW FROST LINE

ROUGH-HEWN DIVIDER FENCE

Your patio or sun deck will take on added importance when you stand this rugged fence beside it. Build it yourself from rough-cut redwood or cedar and then add a colorful jumbo graphic as **a finishing touch. Here, sunlight and breezes stream through the fence openings to keep the deck area cool and bright, yet the tall verticals give a feeling of quiet privacy.**

1 Determine exactly how long you want your fence to be. Figure 2½ inches for each spacer and for each vertical 3x4.

2 Pretreat the 3x4 support posts with penta and allow to dry completely. For the size divider fence shown in the photo, you'll need to set four posts.

3 Dig the postholes, measuring carefully to ensure correct location of each of the support posts. Insert a 3x4 post into each of the holes and anchor in concrete (see instructions for setting posts on page 88).

4 Nail two 2x6 rails to the support posts as shown in the sketch.

5 Cut as many 6-inch-long spacers from redwood 3x4s as you'll need to finish your fence.

6 Glue and nail the first two spacers into position against the first support post (see sketch). Then, butt a vertical redwood 3x4 against the spacers, gluing and nailing it both to the spacers and to the 2x6 rails. Continue for the rest of the fence, alternating spacers and vertical 3x4s.

7 Paint or stain the fence. If you're using rough-hewn lumber, you can keep the natural look by staining the fence or by treating it with weathering oil.

Materials (for an 11½x6-foot fence):

2x6 redwood or cedar—24 ft.
    2 12 ft.
3x4 redwood or cedar—214 feet
    4 9 ft. 6 in.
    24 72 in.
    54 6 in.
Exterior glue, penta, and paint, stain, or weathering oil.

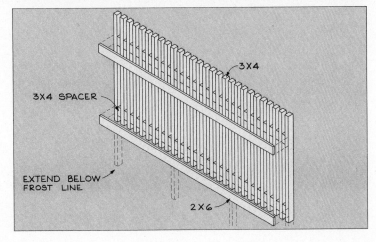

3X4

3X4 SPACER

EXTEND BELOW FROST LINE

2X6

ZIGZAG PRIVACY FENCE

Backyard nooks and crannies offer all kinds of interesting landscaping possibilities. And, that's the beauty of this zigzag sectional privacy fence—you can hopscotch it along your lot line to add new architectural appeal to your property. It's a great way to conceal irregularities in the shape of your lawn, too. Best of all, it's inexpensive to construct.

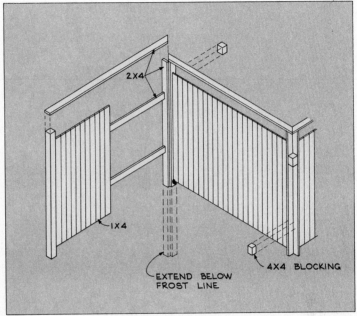

1 Determine how long you want each section of your fence to be. Figure 3½ inches for each 4x4 support, 1½ inches for each 2x4 support, and 3½ inches for each 1x4 slat. (Use 4x4 supports in place of 2x4s on either end of the fence for extra strength.)

2 Plan the locations of your support posts and dig postholes. Treat 4x4 and 2x4 support posts with penta; allow to dry. Insert posts and anchor in concrete (see instructions on page 88).

3 To build one end section of fencing, butt 2x4 rails against the support posts and nail into place (see sketch). Miter one corner of the top rail at a 45-degree angle as shown and nail to the top of the support posts.

4 Nail 1x4 redwood slats to the 2x4 rails. You can butt them one against the other or space them at regular intervals.

5 Construct the remaining sections similarly. Join fence sections by nailing two 4x4 blocks between the supports (see sketch).

6 Paint, stain, or treat the fence with weathering oil.

Materials (8x6-foot end section):
4x4 redwood—12 ft.
    1 10 ft. 6 in.   2 4 in.
2x4 redwood—50 ft.
    2 10 ft. 6 in.   2 91 in.
    1 99½ in.
1x4 redwood—156 ft.
    26 72 in.
Penta, and stain, exterior paint, or weathering oil.

FENCING WITH FIBER GLASS

Want to build a tall fence that still lets in plenty of sunshine? Use fiber glass panels! They pop into place and allow diffused light to shower over plants and shrubs. Here, an exposed aggregate patio is landscaped with large ferns and tree-like shrubs to help "soften" the look. Benches and fence sections are painted contrasting colors to set off the foliage.

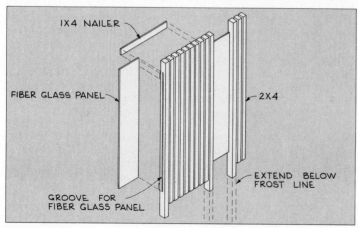

1X4 NAILER

FIBER GLASS PANEL

GROOVE FOR FIBER GLASS PANEL

2X4

EXTEND BELOW FROST LINE

1 Determine how long you want your fence to be. For the style of fence pictured, allow 28 inches for each wood section and 11½ inches for each fiber glass panel.
2 Dig the postholes. (Locate any two posts that support a fiber glass panel ½ inch closer together than the width of the fiber glass panel.)
3 Before you set the 2x4 posts in the ground, use a router or a circular saw to cut a vertical groove ⅛ inch wide and ¼ inch deep on one side of each support post. Start six inches from the top of the post and extend the groove for five feet. Pretreat the bottom of each post with penta and allow to dry.
4 Insert the posts into postholes and anchor in concrete (see instructions on page 88).
5 Align 1x4 redwood nailers as shown and nail them to the 2x4 uprights. Then, at intervals of about one inch, nail 2x4 redwood verticals into position.
6 Before installing fiber glass panels, paint or stain each wood section and support post or treat with weathering oil. Allow to dry.
7 Bend fiber glass panels and pop them into precut grooves in 2x4 uprights (see sketch). Don't worry about breaking panels while bending them; they're flexible.

Materials (for two 2x4 assemblies and one fiber glass panel):
2x4 redwood—136 ft.
    4 10 ft.
  16 72 in.
1x4 redwood—10 ft.
    4 28 in.
One 1x5-foot fiber glass panel, penta, and stain, paint, or weathering oil.

EASY-DOES-IT PLYWOOD PANEL FENCE

Get away from it all behind this privacy screen constructed from colorful plywood panels and a redwood frame. You can build it in a hurry—each panel hangs within a 2x4 "window."

And, for a fence that changes with the seasons, simply paint the removable panels different colors and then rearrange them to form interesting geometric designs.

1 First determine the location and length of your fence. For the type shown, allow 42¾ inches between each 4x4 support post (each 4x4 measures 3½ inches wide).

2 Dig postholes in the proper positions. Treat the 4x4 posts with penta; allow to dry. Insert each 4x4 support into a posthole and anchor in concrete (see instructions on page 88).

3 Nail a 2x4 redwood rail across the top of the 4x4s.

4 Construct the remainder of the redwood frame section-by-section (see sketch).

5 Paint, stain, or treat the redwood frame with weathering oil.

6 Cut enough panels to construct fence and paint various colors.

7 Cut a groove ¼ inch wide and ⅜ inch deep in a redwood 1x1. Then, cut the 1x1 into blocks about 3 inches long. Paint or stain blocks and nail them onto the fence framework as indicated.

8 To hang each plywood panel, first turn an eye screw into one edge of the plywood. Secure the panel by slipping it into the grooved 1x1 block and hanging it from an eye hook screwed into the 2x4 frame (see sketch).

Materials (for an 8x4-foot fence):
2x4 redwood—32 ft.
  2 41 in.   4 20⅝ in.
  2 42¾ in.   1 96 in.
4x4 redwood—24 ft.
  3 90 in.
1x1 redwood—2 ft.
  8 3 in.
¼-inch exterior plywood—1 sht.
  8 18x19 in.
Eight eye screws and hooks, glue, penta, stain, and paint.

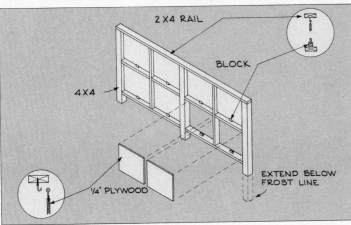

2 X 4 RAIL

BLOCK

4 X 4

¼" PLYWOOD

EXTEND BELOW FROST LINE

BUILDING BASICS YOU SHOULD KNOW

Have you ever heard the saying, "It's not hard once you know how to do it"? Well it's true, especially when it comes to building projects for your home. Once you've mastered the basics, each project you do becomes a series of accomplishable steps rather than a major undertaking.

So, do yourself a favor and spend a few minutes learning about the steppingstones to professional-looking projects. It'll be worth your while.

COMMON CONSTRUCTION MATERIALS

The materials you use for construction will vary, depending on the item's intended use. So when making your selection, ask yourself these questions: Are you constructing something for indoor or outdoor use? Is the item strictly utilitarian, or will it be suitable for use in a living room? Is it intended for light-duty use, or will it be a long-lived project subject to considerable use—and abuse?

Hardboard

Hardboard is available in 4x8-foot sheets and comes in ⅛- and ¼-inch thicknesses. Standard hardboard is an excellent choice for cabinetwork, drawer bottoms, and concealed panels.

You can also get hardboard perforated with holes spaced about one inch apart. Perforated hardboard is recommended for building storage for soiled laundry and for the backs of hi-fi cabinets. The quarter- and eighth-inch perforated hardboard lends itself to storing garden equipment and tools, too, as its holes accept hooks designed for this purpose. To expand or change the arrangement, just switch the hooks around. If the project will be subject to dampness, use tempered hardboard.

Particle board, chip board, and flake board, also members of the hardboard family, have a coarser grain structure, are lighter in color, and are available in thicknesses up to ¾ inch. These products are made of granulated or shredded wood particles forced together under pressure with a binder at high temperatures.

Plywood

Plywood also comes in 4x8-foot sheets, though larger sheets are available on special order. Thicknesses range from ⅛-inch to ¾-inch. For light-duty storage, the ¼- and ½-inch thicknesses are adequate. If you are planning to build an outdoor storage unit, specify *exterior grade* when making your purchase. Exterior grade plywood has its layers glued together with a waterproof glue to withstand rain.

The surfaces of plywood sheets are graded A, B, C, and D—with A the smoother, better surface and D the least desirable appearance. Choose AA (top grade, both sides) only for projects where both sides will be exposed; use a less expensive combination for others.

Solid Wood

Plain, ordinary wood still ranks as the most popular building material. Wood is sold by the "board foot" (1x12x12 inches). One board foot equals the surface area of one square foot, with a nominal thickness of one inch.

Wood is marketed by "grade." For most building projects No. 2 grade will satisfy your needs. This grade may have some blemishes, such as loose knots, but these don't reduce the strength of the wood.

If you're planning to build a unit that will be part of a room's decor, buy *select lumber*—a grade that's relatively free of blemishes.

Remember, too, that outdoor projects are a different subject. Redwood or cedar is preferable, but if you use a soft wood, be sure to treat it for moisture resistance.

Wood is divided into two categories. Softwoods come from trees that don't shed their leaves in the winter: hemlock, fir, pine, spruce, and similar evergreen cone-bearing trees. Hardwoods come from trees that do shed their leaves: maple, oak, birch, mahogany, walnut, and other broad-leaved varieties.

Wood is sold either as dimension lumber or millwork lumber, dimension being used for general construction, and millwork for some furniture building and other special uses.

Also keep in mind that lumber is sold by nominal size. A 2x4, for example, measures 1½x3½ inches. And a piece of ¾ material is less than 1¼ inches thick after milling.

The drawing shows nominal and actual sizes of most common pieces of dimension lumber. Ask lumberyard personnel for help with millwork lumber.

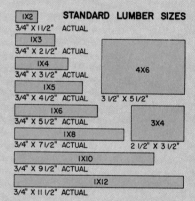

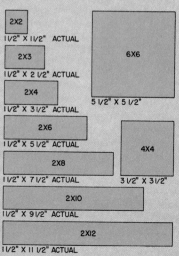

STANDARD LUMBER SIZES

1X2 — 3/4" X 1 1/2" ACTUAL
1X3 — 3/4" X 2 1/2" ACTUAL
1X4 — 3/4" X 3 1/2" ACTUAL
1X5 — 3/4" X 4 1/2" ACTUAL
1X6 — 3/4" X 5 1/2" ACTUAL
1X8 — 3/4" X 7 1/2" ACTUAL
1X10 — 3/4" X 9 1/2" ACTUAL
1X12 — 3/4" X 11 1/2" ACTUAL

4X6 — 3 1/2" X 5 1/2"
3X4 — 2 1/2" X 3 1/2"

2X2 — 1 1/2" X 1 1/2" ACTUAL
2X3 — 1 1/2" X 2 1/2" ACTUAL
2X4 — 1 1/2" X 3 1/2" ACTUAL
2X6 — 1 1/2" X 5 1/2" ACTUAL
2X8 — 1 1/2" X 7 1/2" ACTUAL
2X10 — 1 1/2" X 9 1/2" ACTUAL
2X12 — 1 1/2" X 11 1/2" ACTUAL

6X6 — 5 1/2" X 5 1/2"
4X4 — 3 1/2" X 3 1/2"

OUTDOOR PROJECT POINTERS

Let's face it! Projects that you plan to keep outside will have it pretty rough. If they're not baking in the sun, they'll be trying to fight off the effects of a rainstorm — or worse yet, snow. You can make things easier, though, by first realizing this, then doing something about it. Consider the following tips:

Outdoor Furniture

Traditionally, redwood, cypress, and cedar have been used for garden and patio furniture. However, the weather-resistant qualities of even these excellent woods will leach out after a few years and they'll become weatherbeaten. What to do?

One easy solution is to apply a stain that will still allow the grain to show, but a better bet is two coats of exterior enamel paint. Thin the first coat with turps—if it's an alkyd paint—and apply the second coat without thinning.
Construction. Needless to say, you should always use waterproof glue in the construction of outdoor furniture. If the patio chairs and chaises are to be left in their natural state—unpainted—it's best to use galvanized or aluminum nails, or brass screws for fastening. However, if you plan to paint you can use steel nails, screws, and bolts.

When building a patio table or bench, allow for drainage. A good way to do this is to space the boards ⅜ inch apart.
Rot. A potential weak point in all outdoor furniture is the legs. Because they're constantly immersed in water after a rainfall and during snowstorms, legs draw moisture into the end grain. A simple remedy for this is to install plastic glides to cover the bottom of each leg.

Lighting

Good outdoor lighting will greatly increase the time that you can enjoy your backyard and garden. But, be sure to observe the following rules: If the power line is to be buried underground, make sure that it's the kind approved for burial. It should have a grounding wire, and all outlets to the line should be of the grounding type. And also make sure that any tools or appliances you use outdoors have a three-prong plug that automatically grounds them.
Low-voltage lighting. To avoid any possibility of shock hazard, consider low-voltage lighting, which operates safely on 24 volts supplied by a transformer.
Ground fault interrupter. This device turns off the electric current within 1/50 second after you touch an appliance that has become "shocking." One kind of interrupter plugs into any wall outlet and then receives the individual appliance or extension wire. A more permanent type is installed at the fuse or circuit breaker box.

Concrete Work

Wait for good weather before starting your project. However, if you start a job and the temperature drops to freezing despite what the weatherman said, protect the newly laid concrete from freezing by covering it with burlap, rags, and newspapers. The same procedure applies during extremely hot weather.

Concrete less than an inch thick has little strength. But you can use a thin layer to repair chipped steps or sidewalks if you first apply a bonding agent to the existing concrete.

Always use a "rich" mix for patching work—two parts of clean sand to one part of portland cement. For most other, a 3:2:1 mix is satisfactory (three parts gravel, two parts sand, and one part cement).

Use the chart shown here to figure out how much concrete you will need for a given job. For a small job, you can buy dry ready-mixed concrete in bags; all you need do is add water.

If you need more than two cubic yards, consider purchasing wet ready-mixed concrete. This will arrive at the pouring site in a truck and will be dumped where you indicate. So make sure the forms are ready when the truck arrives (most concrete companies charge extra if you make them wait). It's best to have a neighbor or friend on hand to help you with the job, too.

When setting a fence post into concrete, make sure that the bottom of the post does not project beyond the concrete into the earth. The concrete should be below the frost line and at least four inches above grade. Slope it away from the post for drainage purposes, and use black asphalt roofing cement to seal junctures where post and concrete meet. Fence posts should be 4x4s—nothing lighter.

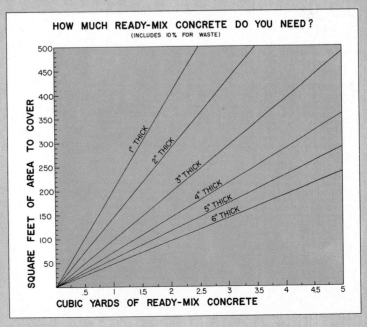

HOW MUCH READY-MIX CONCRETE DO YOU NEED?
(INCLUDES 10% FOR WASTE)

HOW TO BUILD A FENCE

There's nothing like a fence to proclaim, "This is my little corner of the world." And, if built with a little care, a fence will serve you well for years.

Planning the Job

Whether built for privacy or for protection, a fence can become an integral part of your home's landscape. So, you should plan accordingly.

A privacy fence should be high enough to prevent passersby from looking into your grounds and windows. A fence built for protection should be strong enough to prevent animals from entering the grounds and to keep youngsters confined to the yard. It may not stop human intruders, but at least it will discourage them.

The first thing you need to do after you've decided to build a fence is to check the boundary lines of your property to avoid encroachment on your neighbor's lot. Professional fence installers often recommend building a fence six inches within your property lines to avoid possible hassles due to a faulty survey.

You'll need 4x4-inch posts at each end, at each side of any gates, and at intermediate intervals every six feet. For lightweight fencing, such as latticework, intermediate posts set every eight feet will suffice.

Redwood and cedar are traditionally used for fence posts because of their excellent resistance to rot and weather. However, you can use other wood provided you treat it with "penta" (pentachlorophenol), a chemical solution applied by generous brushing or dipping.

A creosote application below ground level and painting above ground level also will help to preserve the posts. Some lumberyards can supply pretreated lumber on order.

After determining how much lumber you need, arrange for the delivery of the posts—and if possible, for the fencing a few days later. If you set the posts in concrete, which is advisable, allow a few days to elapse—even a

week—before starting the actual installation of the fence.

Inasmuch as lumber is commonly sold in 12-, 14-, and 16-foot lengths, plan to set the posts at 6-, 7-, or 8- foot intervals. By doing this you can cut in half the lumber that you buy for the horizontal part of the fence without any waste.

Setting the Posts

Having established the boundary lines of your property, drive a stake at each end, tie a heavy cord between the stakes, and draw it tight. Next, measure off the post intervals—and a gate, if required—and drive in stakes to indicate where you're going to dig the postholes.

If the soil is fairly free of rocks, use a posthole auger. This is like an oversized carpenter's auger with an eight-inch span; a smaller size with a six-inch span also is available. Use the smaller size only if the post is not to be set in concrete. Dig the hole deep enough to avoid heaving due to frost. (Frost lines vary all over the country, so be sure to check with a builder or architect to find out how deep it is in your area.)

If the soil is rocky, you'll have to resort to a clamshell posthole digger (see sketch). If you encounter large rocks, you don't need to move to a new location. A crowbar, sledge, and cold chisel will help.

But if the rock turns out to be as big as a house, don't try to dig it out. Instead, use a star drill and a sledge to drill a hole in the rock to a depth of five inches or so. Fill the hole with concrete (sand and cement, no stones) and force a 12-inch-long steel rod into the concrete-filled hole. Leave it and continue with the rest of the postholes. After the concrete has set, it's safe to install the post at this problem spot. Drill a slightly undersize hole in the bottom of the post and drive it onto the rod.

You can set posts directly into the holes if you first treat them with a penta solution or creosote to prevent rot. Generously brush either solution over the post, or better yet, make a trough in which you can immerse the posts overnight (this procedure ensures sufficient coverage). If you use a brush, pay particular attention to the bottoms of the posts, as this is where water can do the greatest damage.

There are four methods of setting posts. You can set and hold them in place by tamping the soil firmly around the post; by nailing cleats across the below-ground parts of the post; by pouring a collar of concrete around the post and shaping it to drain off water; or by setting the post into concrete.

For light-duty fences, if the soil is sufficiently firm and the hole you have dug has about the same diameter as the post, it's safe to use the first method. Fill the bottom of the hole with coarse gravel or small rocks to a depth of two inches for drainage. Next, set your post. Fill the hole part way with earth, tamp it down firmly, and continue filling and tamping.

Cleats nailed across the post will, of course, require a considerably wider hole, but you can employ the same tamping and filling procedure.

If you decide to use the third method, form a slight depression around the post and pour concrete around it. When the concrete has started to set, shape it so it will shed water.

The last method—setting the post in concrete—is the preferred one if you're after the best results and if time and the added cost of the concrete will permit. The hole in which the concrete is to be poured should be at least four inches wider in diameter than the post.

If the soil in which you have dug the hole is fairly firm, you can use the sides of the hole as the "form." However, if the soil is sandy, or otherwise unstable, make a form for the concrete; it's merely a four-sided open box.

The concrete mix. Use a 3:2:1 mix for the concrete (three parts of gravel or small rocks, two parts of sand, and one part of portland cement). Use a wheelbarrow, a tub, or even a large piece of plywood as a mixing "bowl."

Mix the gravel, sand, and cement thoroughly with a hoe or shovel. Make a depression in the middle of the pile and add clean water. Use the hoe to bring up the mix from the outside of the pile into the water.

Add water a little at a time, *only if necessary*. More concrete is spoiled by too much water than by too little water. The completely mixed mass should have a "heavy" consistency. Any visible water means that you have added too much. If so, add more sand and cement and *keep mixing thoroughly*.

When setting the posts, make sure that you don't force the bottoms beyond the concrete and into the earth. The concrete should be four inches above grade and sloped to drain off rain and snow.

Aligning the posts. Having set the posts in one of the four methods described, the next (and most important) step is to make sure they are in line and absolutely vertical. The first post, or corner post, is the "keystone" with which the next post should be in line. Use the string stretched between the two outside posts as a guide, and a level or a plumb bob to check the "plumb" of the post. Make this check at two adjacent sides of the post and *not at opposite sides*.

After setting each of the posts to the desired height and checking for perpendicularity and alignment, nail outrigger stakes to them to keep them in place while continuing with the rest of the job. It's best to leave the outrigger stakes in place until you have installed the horizontal parts of the fence. Leave posts set in concrete or with a concrete collar undisturbed for a week to allow the concrete to cure. Use this time to decide what style of fence you want, to order the wood, and cut it to size, if necessary.

Fence Designs

The picket fence, by far the most popular and the most traditional, is the simplest fence of all to erect. All it requires are two horizontal rails nailed to the posts, one twelve inches from the ground and the other flush with the post tops so that the tips of the pickets extend six inches above the posts.

Have you ever wondered why picket fences have pointed ends? Good looks, yes. But pointed ends shed water, preventing rot. And it's for this same reason that you should slope tops of your fence posts (see sketch below).

To ensure accurate, uniform spacing of a picket fence, use one of the pickets as a spacer. If you decide you want wider spac-

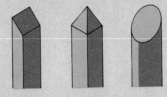

ing, simply cut a piece of scrap wood to the desired width and use it as a spacer.

There are literally dozens of other types of fences you can install, too. The drawing here de-

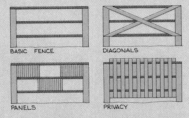

BASIC FENCE   DIAGONALS

PANELS   PRIVACY

picts just a few of the designs you can select for your yard.

And there is no reason why you cannot design a fence to suit your own individual taste. Use one of the basic constructions as a springboard.

Attaching the Rails

Rail installation is just as important as post installation. Before installing the rails, paint all areas of the posts that will be in contact with them. If the fence is to be left unpainted, use a wood preservative. The paint, or preservative, will seal the crevices between the posts and rails, preventing water from seeping in and causing rot.

You can connect the rails to the posts by any of these methods:

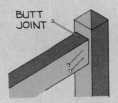

BUTT JOINT

The butt joint. This is the simplest joint of all. The rails are merely toenailed to the sides of the posts as shown. Or, the rails can meet at the top of the post. It's best if you use annular or ring type nails here, as the end grain of a post has woefully little gripping power.

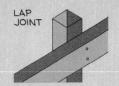

LAP JOINT

The lap joint. Here, the rails are nailed to the sides of the posts. A butted lap joint will be required in those situations when two rails meet. Rails should always meet at a post, not at some point between posts.

Neither the butt joint nor the lap joint requires any preparation of the posts. However, when making any of the following types of joints, prepare the posts before setting them, as it is easier to cut some of the openings beforehand rather than "in the field."

DADO JOINT

The dado joint. Cut away part of the post so that the rail will be flush (or nearly flush) with the post (as shown).

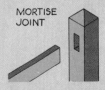

MORTISE JOINT

The mortise joint. This is a more elegant joint and requires cutting a hole in the post (the mortise) to accept the rail. The rails will meet at every other post to make a butt connection *inside* the mortise (assuming the posts are six feet apart and the rails are 12 feet long).

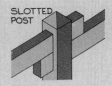

SLOTTED POST

Slotted posts. This is a variation of the mortise joint (see sketch on previous page). In this case, cut the mortise high enough to accept two rails at their junction. This type of joint gives more support to the rails than the mortise joint, as part of each rail projects beyond the opening. Use this joint only at every other post.

RABBET JOINT

MITER JOINT

Corner joints. When the fence turns a corner, you can use any one of the above joints as well as a miter joint or a rabbet joint as indicated above.

Gates

Gates, like front doors, indicate the character of the owner and add to—or subtract from—the decor of the house. Because a gate takes a beating, pay special attention to the posts on either side. Make sure they are solidly set into the ground. As a decorative touch, they can be higher than the posts used for the rest of the fence. And the gate, incidentally, can be higher, or even lower than the fence—it's all a matter of taste.

Typical easy-to-build gates are shown in the sketch below. Note the use of cross framing to add rigidity to the gates.

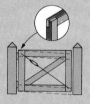

Building the gate. First of all, a gate should be a minimum of three feet wide. Construct the framework, using rabbeted lap joints at all corners (see detail in sketch above). Assemble the frame with galvanized nails, screws, or bolts. An application of waterproof glue will add to the rigidity of the gate.

Install a diagonal for bracing, or a cross brace for extra strength.

Attaching the gate. If you can attach the hinged side of the gate to a side of the house, you're halfway home because the side of

a house is excellent support for a gate. If that's not possible, you'll have to attach it to a separate post.

Hinges for brick. If you can attach your gate to the house, use the hinge shown below. This hinge is installed in the mortar between the bricks. Use a cold chisel and a hammer to make a

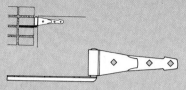

recess for the inside part of the hinge, then force a light concrete or mortar mix into the recess and around the hinge support. Let the concrete dry for a few days before installing the gate.

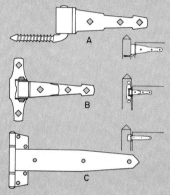

Hinges for wood. You can use any of the hinges shown above to attach hinges to a post. Hinge A has an oversize screw that is threaded into a previously drilled hole in the post. Hinge B is a decorative hinge that is secured to the fence post with two lag bolts. Hinge C is the familiar T-hinge, used for garden gates, garage and barn doors, and any other application requiring a sturdy, functional hinge.

A T-hinge actually reinforces the gate, as the long part of the T covers the gate's corner joint—always a weak area in any gate.

Installing the gate. Having decided where you want the gate and the type of hinges you're going to use, the next step is to hang the gate. First, install the hinges on the gate post (or the side of the house). Make certain that the placement of the hinges will line up with the cross rails of the gate and not at points some-

where in between.

Support the gate on some 2x4s, bricks, or anything else on hand that will raise it to the desired height. Then place the hinge leaves over the gate and mark the holes with a pencil. Drill pilot holes if you're going to use screws, and clearance holes if the job calls for bolts. Use washers under the nuts.

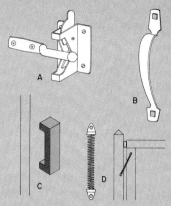

Latches, handles, and springs. In addition to hinges, a gate will require a latch and some sort of handle. Latch A (above) is self-closing. As the gate swings shut, the latch on the post engages the hardware on the gate, effectively keeping the gate closed and preventing it from rattling during a windstorm. Handle B is a store-bought variation of handle A. However, you also can make your own out of some pieces of scrap wood (handle C).

Regardless of whether or not the gate has a latch, a spring to keep it closed is always a good investment. Simply mount it as shown in D, and adjust it for fast or slow closure.

Gate stop. A simple, yet effective door stop will help prevent the hinges from loosening. You can make it from a strip of wood.

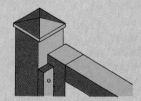

Then, simply screw it to the latch side of the gate. To silence the "bump", you can either line the inside of the strip with some rubber padding or attach a couple of rubber bumpers.

WOOD JOINERY TECHNIQUES

No matter what material you're planning to use, it will have to be cut to size—measure twice and cut once is a good rule—then put together using glue, nails or screws, and one of these joints.

Butt Joints

The simplest joint of all, the butt joint, consists of two pieces of wood meeting at a right angle and

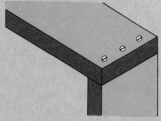

held together with nails, or preferably, screws (see sketch). A dab of glue before using the nails or screws will make the joint even more secure. But don't use glue if you're planning to take the work apart sometime later.

When reinforced by one of the six methods illustrated, the butt joint is effective for making corner

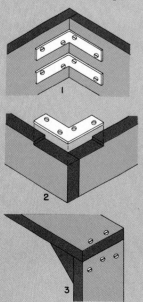

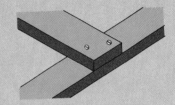

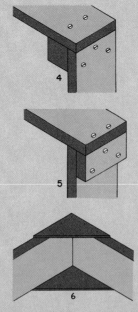

joints. Two common fasteners are angle irons (1), and flat corner plates (2). Using scrap wood, you can reinforce the joint with a triangular wedge (3), or with a square block (4). A variation of the square block places the block on the outside of the joint (5). Finally, a triangular gusset made from plywood or hardboard will also serve to reinforce a corner butt joint (6).

When a butt joint is in the form of a T—for example, in making a framework for light plywood or hardboard—you can reinforce it with an angle iron, T plate, or corrugated fasteners.

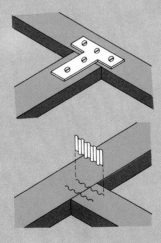

For really rough work, you can drive in a couple of nails at an

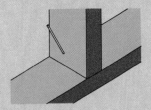

angle, or toenail (see sketch). A variation of this is to place a block of wood alongside the crosspiece and secure it with a couple of nails.

A close cousin to the T joint and the butt joint is the plain overlap joint. It is held in place with at least two screws (see sketch). For extra reinforcement, apply glue between the pieces of wood.

Butt joints are an excellent means of securing backs to various units, especially when appearance is not a factor. Simply cut the back to the outside di-

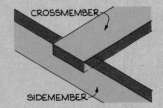

mensions of the work, then nail in place . . . it's called a flush back.

Lap Joints

On those projects where appearance is vital, consider full and half-lap joints. To make a full lap joint, cut a recess in one of the pieces of wood equal in depth to the thickness of the crossmember (see sketch).

The half-lap joint is similar to the full lap joint when finished, but the technique is different. First, cut a recess equal to half the

thickness of the crossmember halfway through the crossrail. Then, make a similar cut in the opposite half of the other piece (see sketch on the next page).

Butt joints and overlap joints do

not require any extra work besides cutting the pieces to size. However, full and half-lap joints

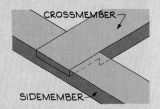

require the use of a backsaw and a chisel. For a full-lap joint, mark off the thickness and width of the crossmember on the work in which it is to fit.

Use the backsaw to make a cut at each end that's equal to the thickness of the crossmember, then use a chisel to remove the wood between the backsaw cuts. Check for sufficient depth and finish off with a fine rasp or sandpaper. Apply white glue to the mating surfaces and insert two screws to hold the joint securely.

Dado Joints

The dado joint is a simple way of suspending a shelf from its side supports. To make a dado joint, draw two parallel lines with a knife

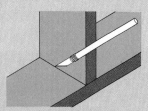

across the face of the work equal to the thickness of the wood it is to engage (see sketch). The depth should be about one-third of the thickness of the wood.

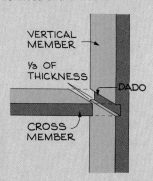

Next, make cuts on these lines and one or more between the lines

with a backsaw. Then, chisel out the wood to the correct depth.

You can speed the job immeasurably by using a router, a bench saw, or a radial arm saw. Any one of these power tools makes the cutting of dadoes an easy job — and provides much greater accuracy than can be achieved by hand.

If appearance is a factor, consider the stopped dado joint. In this type of joint, the dado (the cutaway part) extends only part way, and only a part of the shelf is cut away to match the non-cut part of the dado.

To make a stopped dado, first make your guide marks and chisel away a small area at the stopped end to allow for saw movement. Then make saw cuts

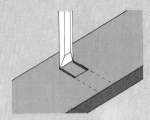

along your guide marks to the proper depth. Next chisel out the waste wood as shown in sketch.

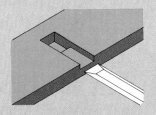

And finally, cut away a corner of the connecting board to accommodate the stopped dado.

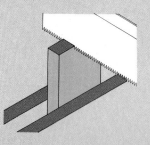

Rabbet Joints

The rabbet joint is really a partial dado. As you can see in the drawing, only one of the meeting members is cut away. It's a simple

joint and, of course, should be secured with nails or screws and glue.

The backs of many units are rabbeted for the best appearance

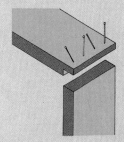

(called inset backs). To make this joint, carefully measure the distance between the rabbeted openings and cut the back accordingly. Then, use thin screws to secure the back to the unit.

Mortise and Tenon Joints

A particularly strong joint, the mortise and tenon joint is excellent when used for making T joints, right-angle joints, and for joints in the middle of rails. As its name indicates, this joint has two parts—the *mortise,* which is the open part of the joint, and the *tenon,* the part that fits into the mortise (see sketch).

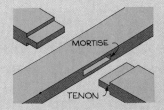

Make the mortise first, as it is much easier to fit the tenon to the mortise than the other way around. Divide the rail (the part to be mortised) into thirds and carefully mark off the depth and the width of the opening with a sharp pencil.

Next, use a chisel, equal to the width of the mortise, to remove the wood between the pencil marks. You can expedite this job by drilling a series of holes in the rail with an electric drill, a drill press, or even a hand drill. (If you have a drill press, you can purchase a special mortising bit that will drill square holes, believe it or not.) Mark the drill bit with a bit of tape to indicate the desired depth. Now use the chisel to remove the excess wood.

To make the tenon, divide the rail into thirds, mark the required depth, and use a backsaw to remove unwanted wood. If you have a bench or radial saw, the job of removing the wood will be much easier. Use a dado blade and set the blades high enough to remove the outer third of the wood. Reverse the work and remove the lower third, leaving the inner third intact.

To assemble, make a trial fit, and if all is well, apply some white glue to the tenon and insert it into the mortise. If by chance the tenon is too small for the mortise, simply insert hardwood wedges at top and bottom.

Use moderate clamping pressure on the joint until the glue dries overnight. Too much pressure will squeeze out the glue, actually weakening the joint.

Miter Joints

You can join two pieces of wood meeting at a right angle rather elegantly with a miter joint. And it's not a difficult joint to make. All you need is a miter box and a backsaw, or a power saw that you can adjust to cut at a 45 degree angle.

Since the simple miter joint is a surface joint with no shoulders for support, you must reinforce it. The easiest way to do this is with nails and glue (see sketch). You'll notice that most picture frames are made this way.

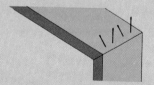

However, for cabinet and furniture work, you may use other means of reinforcement. One way is to use a hardwood spline as shown in the drawing. Apply glue to the spline and to the mitered

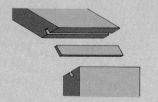

area and clamp as shown until the glue dries.

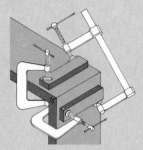

A variation of the long spline uses several short splines—at least three—inserted at opposing angles.

Dowels are a popular method of reinforcing a mitered joint, too. Careful drilling of the holes is necessary to make certain the dowel holes align. Use dowels that are slightly shorter than the holes they are to enter to allow for glue at the bottom. Score or roughen the

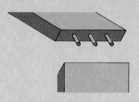

dowels to give the glue a better surface for a strong bond.

Dovetail Joints

The dovetail joint is a sign of good craftsmanship. It's a strong joint especially good for work subject to heavy loads.

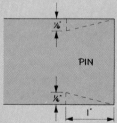

To make the joint, first draw the outline of the pin as shown and cut away the excess wood with a sharp backsaw. Place the pin over the second piece of wood and draw its outline with a sharp pencil. Make the two side cuts with the backsaw and an additional cut or two to facilitate the next step—chiseling away the excess wood. Then test for fit, apply glue and clamp the pieces until

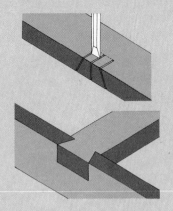

dry. This is the basic way to make most dovetail joints. However, it's much easier to make dovetail joints with a router and dovetail template, especially made for home craftsman use.

Mitered Dovetail Joints

As its name implies, this joint—sometimes called a *secret miter*—combines a miter with a dovetail. It is an exacting joint to make, and like the dovetail joint, a mark of true craftsmanship. The first step is to miter-cut the two pieces of wood to be joined at a 45 degree angle. Then cut away the

pins and the dovetails as shown. Be careful to make all openings between the pins and dovetails the same depth.

Corner Joints

These joints are used for attaching legs to corners for framing. A good technique for joining corners is the three-way joint involving a set of steel braces you can buy. First, insert the bolt into the inside corner of the leg. Then cut slots into the side members, and secure the brace with two screws at each end. Finally, tighten the wing nut.

A variation of the three-way joint uses dowels and a triangular ¾-inch-thick gusset plate for additional reinforcement. To make this joint, first glue the dowels in

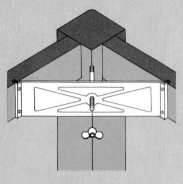

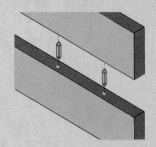

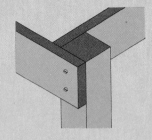

of being fastened to each other, the butted members are each

fastened to the corner post with screws.

Edge-to-Edge Joints

Whenever an extra-wide surface is required, such as a desk top, workbench, or a large storage cabinet, this joint fills the bill. To make it, glue together two or more boards, then hold securely with either bar or pipe clamps. If the boards have a pronounced grain, reverse them side-to-side

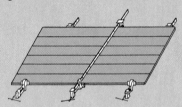

to minimize warping. For additional strength, screw cleats to the underside of the boards.

You also can use hardwood splines to join several boards. Cut a groove the exact width of the spline along the meeting sides of the two boards (see sketch). Cut the grooves slightly deeper than the spline width and in the exact center of the board thickness. The best way to cut such grooves is with a router or a bench saw.

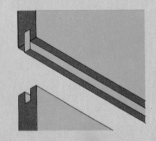

Then assemble with glue and clamps.

Another possibility for joining several boards involves the use of dowels. To make this joint, first

make holes in the boards. You can either use a doweling jig or a drill. If you use a drill, first drive

brads (small finishing nails) into one board and press them against the second board to leave marks for drilling. Make the dowel holes slightly deeper than the dowels. Score the dowels, apply glue, join the two boards together, and clamp with pipe or bar clamps until the glue sets (allow plenty of time).

If you'll be drilling many dowel holes, you may want to use a wood or metal template to ensure accurate spacing.

Box Joints

One joint is so common in the construction of boxes — and drawers — it's called a *box joint,* or a *finger joint because its parts* look like the outstretched fingers of a hand (see sketch). Note that one of the mating pieces must have two end fingers, or one more

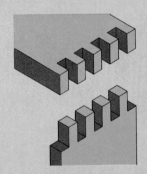

finger than the piece it is to engage. You can make this joint by hand with a backsaw and a small, sharp chisel. However, it is much easier, quicker, and more accurate to make it on a bench saw. Use a dado blade set to the desired width and proper depth of the fingers and mark off the waste area so there will be no mistake as to what you want to cut away.

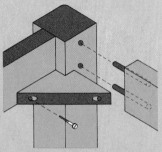

the vertical piece (see sketch). Let them dry completely, then finish the assembly.

A glued miter joint, reinforced with screws and glue, also makes a good corner joint. Make sure the screws do not penetrate the outside surface of the mitered joint.

Probably the strongest of the corner joints is the mortise and tenon (with mitered ends) reinforced with screws (see sketch). The miters on the ends of the tenons allow for a buildup of glue in the mortise, which in turn makes the joint stronger. Make sure that the holes you drill for the screws are not in line with each other.

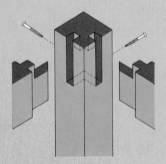

Otherwise, the wood may split. Use flathead screws and countersink the holes.

The simplest corner joint of all is a butt joint for the two horizontal members (see sketch). Instead

THE HARDWARE YOU'LL NEED

For any sort of fastening work, you will need nails, screws, and bolts, as well as glues and cements.

Nails, Screws, and Bolts

These most common of all fastening materials are available in diverse widths and lengths, and in steel, brass, aluminum, copper, and even stainless steel.

Nails. Nails are sold by the penny—which has nothing to do with their cost. The "penny," (abbreviated *d*) refers to the size. The chart shows a box nail marked in the penny size designations as well as actual lengths in inches.

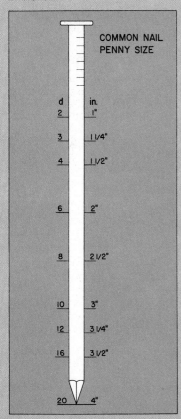

d	in.
2	1"
3	1 1/4"
4	1 1/2"
6	2"
8	2 1/2"
10	3"
12	3 1/4"
16	3 1/2"
20	4"

COMMON NAIL PENNY SIZE

Use common nails for general-purpose work; finish and casing nails for trim or cabinetwork; and brads for attaching molding to walls and furniture.

COMMON SCREWS

Type	Use
WOOD — Flathead, Roundhead, Ovalhead	For the great majority of fastening wood to wood and other joints.
DOWEL	End joints where one piece of wood can turn.
HANGER	To make dismantle-able joints without a bolt.
LAG	
THREAD FORMER	In thicker metals and in plywood applications.
SELF TAPPING — Solid, Split	In attaching to thinner sheet metals.

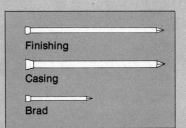

Finishing

Casing

Brad

Screws. Screws are sold by length and diameter. The diameter is indicated by a number, from 1 to 16. The thicker the screw shank, the larger the number. The drawing shows some of the most popular types of screws.

Always drill a pilot hole when inserting a screw into hardwood. And always drill a clearance hole in the leading piece of wood when screwing two pieces of wood together. Without a clearance hole, the leading piece tends to "hang up," preventing a tight fit between the two.

Bolts. You can also fasten wood together with bolts, but only if there is access to the back for the required washer and nut. A bolted joint is stronger than a screwed joint, as the bolt diameter is generally thicker than the comparable screw, and also because the wrench used to tighten the nut can apply much more force than a screwdriver in a screw slot.

Glues and Cements

While not "hardware" as such, glue is an important adjunct to any fastening job. The so-called white glue is excellent for use with wood, and only moderate clamping pressure is required. When dry, it is crystal clear. However, it's not waterproof so don't use it for work subject to excessive dampness—and of course, never for outdoor use. Use the two-tube epoxy "glue" for joints that must be waterproof.

Plastic resin glue, a powder that you mix with water to a creamy consistency, is highly water resistant.

Contact cement provides an excellent bond between wood and wood, and wood and plastic. When working with contact cement, remember that it dries instantly and position your surfaces

COMMON BOLTS

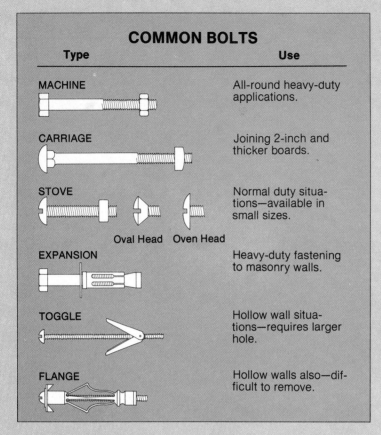

Type	Use
MACHINE	All-round heavy-duty applications.
CARRIAGE	Joining 2-inch and thicker boards.
STOVE — Oval Head / Oven Head	Normal duty situations—available in small sizes.
EXPANSION	Heavy-duty fastening to masonry walls.
TOGGLE	Hollow wall situations—requires larger hole.
FLANGE	Hollow walls also—difficult to remove.

The plate type caster is merely screwed to the bottom by four screws that pass through holes in the plate. They are not height adjustable unless, of course, you use shims.

All casters use ball bearings as part of the plate assembly to facilitate swiveling. For extra-heavy usages, purchase casters with ball-bearing wheels as well.

The wheels on casters are of two types—plastic or rubber. Use casters with plastic wheels if the project is to be rolled on a soft surface such as a rug; rubber wheeled casters are best on hard concrete, vinyl, or hardwood. It's a good idea to use graphite to lubricate the wheels and their bearings, as oil tends to pick up dust and dirt.

To prevent a caster-equipped unit from rolling, get locking casters. A small lever on the outside of the wheel locks a ''brake.'' Brakes on only two of the four casters on a unit are sufficient.

Miscellaneous Hardware

There are many types of hardware that can come in handy when you're constructing storage bins, cabinets, chests, shelves, and other projects.

Following are some you may need from time to time: corrugated fasteners connect two boards or mend splits in wood; angle irons reinforce corners; flat and T plates also reinforce work; masonry nails secure work to concrete or brick walls; steel plates with a threaded center are used for attaching legs to cabinets; screw eyes and cup hooks allow for hanging items inside storage units; and lag screw plugs made of lead or plastic secure furring strips or shelf brackets to masonry walls.

You'll be wise to stock your workshop with most of these items in a couple of sizes. That way, you won't have to make a special trip when they're needed.

When to Use What Glue

Type	Use
White glue (No mixing)	Paper, cloth, wood
Epoxy (requires mixing)	Wood, metal, stone (waterproof)
Plastic resin (requires mixing)	Wood to wood (water resistant)
Contact cement (no mixing)	Wood to wood or plastic (waterproof)
Waterproof glue (requires mixing)	Wood to wood (waterproof)

together exactly as you want them. You won't get a second chance.

True waterproof glue comes in two containers; one holds a liquid resin, the other a powder catalyst. When dry, this glue is absolutely waterproof and can be safely used for garden equipment and all outdoor projects and furniture.

Glides and Casters

The intended use determines whether a piece of furniture needs a caster or a glide. If you don't plan to move it frequently, use a glide; otherwise, a caster is the best choice.

Glides come in many sizes, determined by the glide area touching the floor, and with steel or plastic bottoms. The simple nail-on glides aren't height adjustable but you can adjust screw glides by screwing the glide in or out to prevent wobbling if the floor is uneven, or if by some chance, the project does not have an even base.

Casters are made in two styles—stem type (only the stem type is adjustable) and plate type (at left in sketch). The stem type requires a hole to be drilled into the leg or base of the cabinet or furniture. This hole accepts a sleeve that in turn accepts the stem of the caster.